בס"ד

להורינו וידידינו היקרים

קבלו נא את תשורתנו

כרוכה ביחד עם ברכתנו הלבבית

שתראו נחת מכל משפחתכם

ונזכה ביחד לראות בהרמת קרן התורה

בהכרה והוקרה

הנהלת תיכון בית יעקב

מסורה

The ArtScroll Series®

Rabbi Nosson Scherman / Rabbi Meir Zlotowitz

General Editors

Silence Is

Published by

Mesorah Publications, ltd

Thy Praise

The Life and Ideals of
Rabbanit Batya Karelitz

by Esther Austern

FIRST EDITION
First Impression . . . February, 1990

Published and Distributed by
MESORAH PUBLICATIONS, Ltd.
Brooklyn, New York 11232

Distributed in Israel by
MESORAH MAFITZIM / J. GROSSMAN
Rechov Harav Uziel 117
Jerusalem, Israel

Distributed in Europe by
J. LEHMANN HEBREW BOOKSELLERS
20 Cambridge Terrace
Gateshead, Tyne and Wear
England NE8 1RP

Distributed in Australia & New Zealand by
GOLD'S BOOK & GIFT CO.
36 William Street
Balaclava 3183, Vic., Australia

Distributed in South Africa by
KOLLEL BOOKSHOP
22 Muller Street
Yeoville 2198
Johannesburg, South Africa

THE ARTSCROLL SERIES®
SILENCE IS THY PRAISE
© Copyright 1990, by MESORAH PUBLICATIONS, Ltd.
4401 Second Avenue / Brooklyn, N.Y. 11232 / (718) 921-9000

ISBN
0-89906-568-6 (hard cover)
0-89906-569-4 (paperback)

Typography by Compuscribe at ArtScroll Studios, Ltd.

Printed in the United States of America by Noble Book Press
Bound by Sefercraft, Quality Bookbinders, Ltd. Brooklyn, N.Y.

Table of Contents

ک‌Preface

SHORTLY AFTER ROSH CHODESH ELUL, 1984, Rebbetzin Chana Brodman called me. "I don't have to tell you how important the month of Elul is," she said. "As the *Yamim Noraim* (Days of Awe) are upon us, the Rav has invited the women of Savyon (a fashionable suburb near Tel Aviv) to an important evening of *hisorerus* (inspiration)." I was advised that Rav David Brodman *shlita*, the rabbi of Savyon, would elaborate on the origin and depth of the many inspiring prayers of Rosh Hashanah and Yom Kippur. In addition, he asked that I say a few words to impress upon the women the seriousness of the hour. In view of the short notice, he left the choice of topic to my discretion.

Less than three months had passed since the passing of Rebbetzin Batya Karelitz, ע"ה, and she was still very much part of my thoughts. I decided to speak of Rebbetzin Batya's love of Hashem and her strict adherence to His commandments, of her deep faith and genuine piety, and of her humble, giving heart. The women appeared to be moved.

The High Holidays had long passed when, by chance, one evening I met Rebbetzin Batya's daughter-in-law, Rebbetzin Miriam Karelitz. I told her about the evening in Savyon. She was pleased with the impact her mother-in-law's memory had made upon the women. "If only I could write the story of her life! It could be of significant benefit — a *kiddush Hashem*," I said wistfully. "I do have some writing experience," I continued, as the idea caught my imagination and began to grow and stir within me. "I was but twenty years old when I wrote my first book, *Satan Without His Mask*," I added anxiously, wishing to prove myself. "It was a description of my encounter with Nazi brutality during the Holocaust. *Baruch Hashem*, I married before I had a chance to try and have it published. And then, raising a family took precedence."

Rebbetzin Miriam listened with interest to the idea. She responded, "My mother-in-law detested publicity and fame. She never wanted honor during her lifetime and does not need it now. אֲבָל צָרִיךְ לְזַכּוֹת אוֹתָהּ, *but it is necessary to credit her deeds.* Let's ask Rav Nissim."

We went to see Rav Nissim Karelitz. The rebbetzin opened the door. She was visibly gladdened by our visit. Rebbetzin Miriam informed her sister-in-law of the purpose of our coming. She listened and, after pausing a moment or two, said, "We have to ask the Rav."

The two sisters-in-law walked into Rav Nissim's study. I remained in the outer room. The women were there for some time — at least, so it seemed to me. When they finally emerged, Rebbetzin Leah said, "You have the Rav's permission. The Rav asks only that you write from the heart."

I drove Rebbetzin Miriam home. On the way I asked, "What was the most memorable experience you shared with Rebbetzin Batya, ע"ה?" She told me the story of "The Silver Esrog Box" (see page 138).

I began to interview members of the family. For historical information and family background I was given the first volume of *Pe'er Hador*, the biography of the Chazon Ish, זצ"ל, written by Rav Aharon Sorasky and edited by Rav Shlomo Cohen. Later one of my children asked Rav Sorasky for permission to use the book for reference, and he graciously consented.

The writing, however, did not come easy. A certain fear took hold of me. I was bothered by a nagging conscience that gave me no peace. "Who am I to write of the saintly ways of Rebbetzin

Batya Karelitz, ע"ה?" At one point I asked Rebbetzin Miriam if she knew someone more worthy of such an undertaking.

"No, I don't know anyone," she said. "Besides, the idea was yours. It would never have occurred to us if you had not suggested it."

In my desperation I mustered the courage to ask the Steipler for a *brachah*. Rebbetzin Aliza Zeichner, a devoted friend of the Karelitz family and a *bas bayis* in Rebbetzin Batya's home, accompanied me. The Steipler Gaon's daughter, Rebbetzin Yuspa Barzam, received us warmly. Because the Steipler did not grant audiences to women, Rebbetzin Barzam acted as go-between. We wrote our request on paper and handed it to her.

"The Rav is resting at the moment," Rebbetzin Barzam said, "but don't worry. *B'ezras Hashem*, I will show your note to the Rav. Come back tomorrow morning and I will, *b'ezras Hashem*, have an answer for you."

I did not sleep a wink that night. I imagined a stern, scolding attitude in reaction to my request. But I resolved that come what may I would accept and follow the Steipler Gaon's advice.

The following morning I knocked gently on Rebbetzin Barzam's door. My heart was pounding as she opened it and invited me in. But I wanted the answer in a hurry, and with a quiver in my voice asked, "What did the Steipler Gaon say?"

"*Es vet zein gut* — It will be good."

"What does that mean?" I asked, confused.

"It is a *brachah*," Rebbetzin Barzam explained, smiling.

❀   ❀   ❀

It took four-and-one-half years to write this book. During those years I was in the finest company. Rebbetzin Batya was by my side always. When good tidings came my way, she taught me to be grateful and humble. When times were difficult, she filled me with faith and taught me to count my blessings. Writing about Rebbetzin Batya was in itself an enriching experience which enabled me to reap thereby the fruits of my labor.

A long-time acquaintance advised, "If you want your book

published, it must be entertaining and humorous. Inject lots of humor." But Rebbetzin Batya never meant to entertain. Her ways were thought provoking and her very life a lesson. Certainly she was no conformist. On the contrary, at a time when women of the world worshiped the notion that it was important for the child that the *mother* be happy, Rebbetzin Batya felt that it was important for the mother that her *child* be happy. At a time when the world had become an aimless merry-go-round, Rebbetzin Batya's priorities lay in the relentless search for order and purpose. For that is the way of Hashem.

~§ Title

The title of this book, *Silence Is Thy Praise*, was suggested by Rebbetzin Aliza Zeichner. It is borrowed from a verse in *Tehillim*.

Tehillim is, in the main, a reflection of King David's passionate yearning to sing the praises of Hashem. It is an outpouring of feeling, fervor and awe. "My L-rd, open my lips, that my mouth may declare your praises" (*Tehillim* 51:17). Nevertheless King David realized that there are no words to measure or describe fully the infinite grandeur and omnipotence of the Almighty. He was therefore moved to proclaim, *Silence Is Thy praise* (*Tehillim* 65:1. See *Rashi's* comment).

How does one worship or praise Hashem through silence? The life of Rebbetzin Batya Karelitz provides an answer. Her life was the epitome of silent and unobtrusive praise of Hashem.

~§ Pictures

Women may wonder with justification why there are so few pictures of women in a book about a rebbetzin. I had an impressive collection of appropriate photographs, but I learned that some women of the Karelitz family felt that their mother and aunts would not have wanted the pictures to be published. In deference to their wish, I returned all the pictures except those of Rebbetzin

Batya, her mother and her paternal grandmother. These three generations had a common outlook on life and the same love for Torah and Jewish heritage. Their photographs portray three strong and continuous links in the chain of Jewish history.

∾§ Acknowledgments

I thank Hashem for granting me life and enabling me to reach this day.

I shall be eternally grateful to Rebbetzin Batya Karelitz ע″ה for her warmth, hospitality, and many kindnesses. I was privileged to know her in the final years of her life. She opened my eyes to the ways of the righteous.

I am deeply indebted to Rav Nissim Karelitz, שליט″א, for permitting me to write of his saintly mother. The entire Karelitz family enthusiastically encouraged me in this endeavor. By relating to me personal experiences and anecdotes, they enabled me to gain a perceptive view of Rebbetzin Batya's piety and stature. In this I was particularly aided by Rebbetzin Esther Finkel, her niece. Her penetrating insight inspired me. Whether it was with a twinkle in her eye, a gentle smile or a furrowed brow, she made her point. I gained a vivid picture thereby of life in Kossova. With the aid of her American-born sons-in-law, who read parts of the manuscript, she made valuable suggestions.

Reference to important contributions by Rebbetzins Aliza Zeichner and Batsheva Schwartz of Bnei Brak and Rebbetzin Shoshana Privalsky of Brooklyn is contained in the text. To them all I am sincerely grateful.

The story of the eventful sleigh ride from Vilna to Yehoshua Tanchum's *bris milah* was related to me by Rebbetzin Shulamit Alpha, a daughter of Rav Meir Karelitz זצ″ל. Recalling the incident gave her pleasure, and I thank her for it.

Rav Aharon Sorasky graciously allowed me to use material from *Pe'er Hador*, his multi-volume biography of the Chazon Ish. For this I am greatly indebted.

Mrs. Rose Ann Silecchia typed the manuscript. I truly appreciate her cheerful execution of a tedious task.

I am much indebted to ArtScroll for accepting this book for publication. Rabbi Nosson Scherman was especially patient and understanding and ever ready to be of help. I am most grateful to the entire staff of Mesorah Publications Ltd. Rabbi Meir Zlotowitz and Rabbi Nosson Scherman have honored me by including my work in their impressive roster of publications. Mrs. Judi Dick and Zvi Shapiro edited the manuscript. I admire their dedication, skill and perceptiveness, and I appreciate their great help. I am grateful as well to Mrs. Menucha Silver, Mrs. Zissi Landau, and Bassy Goldstein who typed, and to Mrs. Faygie Weinbaum who proofread the book. Finally, the artistry of Rabbi Shea Brander has become legendary. To him and his assistant, Yitzchok Saftlas, I am very grateful.

My daughter-in-law, Penina Austern, did research, prepared the glossary and made numerous helpful comments, for which I am indeed grateful.

I acknowledge with profound gratitude the tireless work of my husband, Shmuel Ezra Austern. He spent many days correcting and generally polishing the English. His comments and suggestions were indispensable.

To my parents, who implanted in me a love of *Yiddishkeit* and taught me to walk in the paths of Torah, I shall be forever grateful. My father, Yechezkel Shrage Goldschild, יחזקאל שרגא בן משה ז"ל, and my mother Gittel, גיטעל בת הרב נתן ע"ה, perished in the Holocaust. May their memory be blessed!

My short description of Israel's War of Independence is in part a reflection of my personal loss. My only brother, David Goldschild, דוד בן יחזקאל שרגא ז"ל, fell in 1948 at the age of nineteen near Jenin, in an ambush by Iraqi forces. May his memory and that of his fallen comrades be blessed!

E.A.

CHAPTER ONE

The Marriage

"In youth and in love but trembling with fear, the Children of Israel stood at the foot of Mount Sinai and proclaimed: "We shall comply and we shall listen!"

(*Shemos* 24:7)

ITH THIS VOW THE HOLY TORAH was taken in matrimony, and the eternal obligation to honor and obey was ratified. Since that fateful day more than three thousand years ago, Torah, the bride, has never been forsaken.

The Children of Israel and the Torah — united — have survived many raging storms. Together they have withstood the ruthless attacks of countless enemies. In every generation from time immemorial, there have appeared on the scene deadly antagonists, motivated solely by a relentless desire to bring about the dissolution of this marriage. Alien ideologies, purporting to be based upon enlightened reason and invariably clad in either holy garb or ridiculous fantasy, have been skillfully and brutally manipulated with a view toward the separation of the Jew from his Torah.

Despised, ridiculed, persecuted, plundered, beaten and burned, the faithful have never wavered in their devotion. There has too often been a sharp contrast between Scripture's promise of a magnificent, bright future and the bleak torment of reality. Nevertheless, the more severe the affliction or tribulation, the more tenacious the pious Jew's belief, and the more zealous his obedience to *mitzvos*. As a result, no generation of Jews has ever been without learned and righteous sages who painstakingly, steadfastly and selflessly have inspired and guided their people to adhere to a Torah-true way of life. There have always been those who courageously declare:

> Praiseworthy is the people for whom this is so; praiseworthy is the people whose G-d is Hashem ... (*Tehillim* 144:15). But as for me, I trust in Your kindness; my heart will exult in Your salvation (*Tehillim* 13:6).

The spirit of this heritage was most beautifully exemplified in the life of Rebbetzin Batya Karelitz. In our turbulent times she portrayed true Jewish womanhood, quietly exerting a profound influence on the House of Jacob.

CHAPTER TWO

The 25th Day of Sivan

AN HOUR BEFORE DAYBREAK on a warm, clear night in early summer, Rebbetzin Batya Karelitz awoke from a light sleep. She raised her frail body slowly and quietly and sat at the edge of

The Candle Dropped

her bed. Rochel, her teen-age granddaughter, who shared the small room with her, was asleep nearby. The rebbetzin took pains to make as little noise as possible lest she wake Rochel. It was year-end exam time in Rav Wolf's Bais Yaakov Seminary in Bnei Brak, which Rochel attended, and her grandmother was well aware of her need to sleep. Rebbetzin Karelitz was in her ninetieth year. Although physically weak, she nevertheless tried her utmost to lighten the burden of those who cared for her. Often this required an almost superhuman effort.

The window was open and a gentle sea breeze cooled the otherwise warm, humid air. Some light from a street lamp outside penetrated the room, enabling her to make out without difficulty objects around her. One of these was a two-handled plastic mug about five inches in height and the same in diameter, containing water almost to the brim. It lay in a large bowl, also of plastic, located on a small desk adjacent to the bed. Slowly and carefully she grasped the mug and poured its contents onto her hands, interchanging them a number of times.

After thoroughly drying her hands with a towel, she sought a match to light a half-burned candle protruding from a simple copper candlestick on the same desk. In consideration of Rochel, she had opted for the soft glow of candlelight rather than the glare of the electric bulb. No sooner had she managed to kindle the flame than the candlestick with the candle in it dropped with a clatter onto the ceramic-tiled floor, snuffing out the flame. Rochel woke with a start. She immediately sized up the situation, hurriedly washed *negel vasser*, as her grandmother had done, and switched on the electric light.

"What is it, Bobbe?" she asked apprehensively.

"A *bissel vasser*, Rochel — a *bissel vasser*," she whispered, almost inaudibly. Her voice, usually of a soft, gentle and sweet quality, had in it a perceptible tinge of distress. Was it the accidental fall of the candle? Or perhaps her concern for Rochel? Or was it something more serious?

The rebbetzin had suffered for as long as she could remember from a weak heart. Doctors had marveled at her longevity in the face of this condition. What allowed her heart to continue to function and sustain her could not be explained medically. Could a burning spirit alone fire a human heart that had otherwise faltered? Could a burning spirit sustain life above and beyond a reasonable and sound medical prognosis?

Rochel removed the bowl and brought a glass of fresh water. She handed it gently to her grandmother, who nodded in appreciation and asked that the light be switched off.

"Go back to sleep, Rochel," she said. Then in an audible whisper, slowly articulating each word in deliberate concentration, she recited the blessing on water: "Blessed art Thou, Hashem, King of the universe, by Whose word all things come into being."

Rochel answered, "Amen," and the rebbetzin drank. She returned the glass to the desk and said, "Rochel, I need light."

Rochel jumped out of bed and flicked on the switch. When she turned to face her grandmother she saw, to her horror, that her grandmother, who appeared to be bending forward as if in search of her slippers, was about to fall. Not being near enough, she was powerless to be of aid. If only she had asked for her slippers! If only . . .

On that fateful morning, the 25th day of Sivan, 1984, Rebbetzin Batya Karelitz departed this life.

❀ ❀ ❀

REBBETZIN BATYA KARELITZ was born in the Hebrew month of Sivan, and she passed away in the month of Sivan. It is the way of the righteous to so complete the cycle. They live and die *bishleimus* — in symmetrical fulfill-

The Funeral

ment.

The hour of the funeral was no coincidence either. In Israel, two o'clock in the afternoon is the time of day when synagogues are most likely to be silent of prayer and the houses of learning empty of students. It was accordingly an appropriate time for the funeral to take place. This *eishes chayil*, woman of valor, devoutly dedicated to holy worship and sacred learning, would not have wished to interrupt any Divine service. It was fitting that her wish be granted.

The rebbetzin's stretcher was lifted and carried out of the small and unassuming reception room of her home. The formidable crowd that had gathered outside on Yehudah Halevi Street, a narrow, winding, hilly street in the heart of Bnei Brak, had its eyes transfixed on the seemingly weightless stretcher, supported almost effortlessly by several men who had vied to carry her on this last journey.

In her lifetime the rebbetzin had always been extremely careful not to be a burden. She would have wished that it be no less that way in death. It was against her nature to impose herself on or bother others. To her a favor received was regarded as a debt to be repaid as soon as possible. When she died she left no debts — only a host of indebted relatives, friends and acquaintances.

The pallbearers proceeded slowly, followed on foot by a vast multitude of men, a veritable sea of black hats and long, black jackets; and following them, an equally large crowd of quietly sobbing women. The procession crossed Rabbi Akiva Street,

Rav Zalman Rotberg שליט״א

stopping at Kollel Chazon Ish in Zichron Meir at the foot of Rechov Maharshal. This advanced rabbinical seminary had been founded by and was named after the rebbetzin's revered brother, the Chazon Ish. From a second-story balcony, loudspeakers carried the moving eulogies to the throngs stretching several blocks in all directions. The unaffected simplicity of the laments in itself told the story. Rav Zalman Rotberg, a nephew through marriage, and dean of Beit Meir, the Bnei Brak rabbinical seminary named after the rebbetzin's oldest brother, cried, "Oh Batya, Batya ...! Oh! Batya built her home! What a home! Oh! Torah ... Torah ... She was all Torah! Oh! Shabbos ... Shabbos! What Shabbos ! Oh *kashrus*! What *kashrus*! Oh! What righteousness! What virtue! What modesty! Oh! Crown of royalty! Our royal crown!"

The hushed and bereaved assemblage strained to hear every word, not so much to acknowledge the praise that was certainly due, but rather to register a lesson to be learned and an example to be emulated. A stranger to the scene may have wondered with some justification what the fuss was all about. In today's world it is the dynamic woman who is looked up to. Far from shy, she thrives and takes pride in flashy accomplishments. But in religious circles a head-covered woman keeping Shabbos, observing *kashrus* and praying habitually is considered the norm. Countless Orthodox Jewish women behave in the same manner.

In truth the rebbetzin never aspired to extraordinary accomplishments or heroic feats. She did not aim to move the world. She did not lecture, write learned articles or busy herself as an organization *"macher."* She detested ostentatious show and flattery. Indeed, because the lust for fame, honor or grandeur never tarnished her soul, she was blessed with it all. As with a few deft and well-placed strokes of the brush an accomplished artist creates a work of art, so the rebbetzin was endowed with that rare quality that refines and perfects life as only a life refined and perfected by Torah and *mitzvos* can be. This was the dominant and transcending feature of her life: to follow implacably the dictates of the Torah and to gain thereby a crystal-clear understanding of her role as a Jewess.

CHAPTER THREE

Roots, Vigil, Harmony

A righteous man will flourish like a date palm.
Like a cedar in Lebanon he will grow tall.
Planted in the house of Hashem.
In the courtyards of G-d they will flourish.
They will still be fruitful in old age.
Vigorous and fresh they will be.

(Tehillim 92:13-15)

Childhood in the Garden N THE ICY SHORES OF THE BALTIC SEA in unsung Lithuania, far from the glittering capitals of enlightened Europe and totally oblivious to the secular world, a spiritual garden had taken root. Hashem had fertilized the land with poverty and watered it with the many Jewish tears shed through the ages — and it blossomed. As of old, revered Talmudic giants appeared on the scene. Their presence electrified the people and awakened in them a powerful curiosity to know. Like wildfire, the desire to learn Torah inflamed young and old. Institutions of higher learning mushroomed all over Eastern Europe. Vilna, Slobodka, Ponevez, Radin, Volozin, Lomza, Telz and other cities became famous for the *yeshivos* they spawned and nurtured. In these institutions sages and students alike studied the *gemara* and the commentaries, exchanging insights, elucidating, explaining, discussing and arguing, in a grand and ceaseless effort to unravel its complexities. Day and night they dug deep into the intricacies and mysteries of the Talmud and rejoiced with every find. Intense concentration sharpened the mind, warmed the heart and refined the soul. There was abundant quality amidst the quantity. Most amazing, however, was the transcending feeling of urgency that so strongly gripped everyone, as if Jewish survival depended upon it.

Kossova, Rebbetzin Batya's birthplace, was a little village typical of its time and place: lacking prestige, with no claim to fame, very ordinary. Its Jewish inhabitants were, more or less, uniformly poor. The few who were looked upon as affluent were middle class, at best. On the other hand, most of the poor were not destitute. Somehow, from day to day, they managed to eke out a meager living and to provide themselves with life's necessities. They were comfortably poor. In any event, poverty seemed to have no adverse effect upon the Jewish community as long as they were enwrapped in the spiritual bliss that characterized Jewish life in Eastern Europe. The Jews of Kossova, like those of other *shtetls*, were feverishly involved in the common effort to forge and promote a higher standard of *Yiddishkeit*. Ere long Kossova gained renown, due to its learned and righteous rav, Rabbi Shmaryahu Yosef Karelitz, and his saintly rebbetzin, Rasha Leah. They raised nine children, each a precious jewel in the royal crown of Torah. So began a royal dynasty, adding prominence to a family already distinguished by a long and solid line of rabbinical ancestors. The eighth child was Batya.

❧ ❧ ❧

HEAPS OF FRESH CHERRIES, PEACHES, PLUMS and a variety of berries, all now out of season, had been reduced to jarred preserves lining the pantry shelves of Kossova.

No Lashon Hara   However, the trees were still heavy with sun-ripened apples and pears, which the farmers hastened to harvest lest an early frost damage the fruit. The September sky was cloudless, but a chill in the air portended the approach of a long winter.

Little Bashl, as Batya was lovingly nicknamed, accompanied her older sisters to the market place. Only six years old, she scampered along, half running, half skipping, to keep up. It was not that her sisters were inconsiderate of her. They simply rushed out of habit rather than the need of the moment. To them an errand was not a pleasure outing. Their mother had always impressed the value of time upon them. Time was a commodity to be guarded zealously. It was a gift from Above, something never to be wasted. Fine Jewish girls must always have something worthwhile to do.

From early childhood they were taught that idleness was a breeder of evil. Not the least of its consequences was the tendency to indulge in needless talk, in gossip and even slander — all tools of Satan. They were likewise trained to turn a deaf ear to street talk and the commonplace, vehicles as they were for uncouth and occasionally vulgar language.

Bashl left the shopping to her sisters, and she looked upon and listened to the bewildering scene with curiosity and interest: the boisterous bargaining between vendors and customers, the neighing of horses and the clatter of their hooves on the cobblestone pavement, the shouts of the draymen, the screams of the women and the giggles of young girls — all fusing into a cacophony of discordant sound. In the midst of the tumult Bashl's alert little ears suddenly picked up a most derogatory and degrading piece of gossip. It stunned and pained her. Without a word to her sisters she abruptly took off and ran all the way home. She proceeded directly to her father's study, pausing briefly at the door to catch her breath. Her heart still pounding, she forced restraint and waited. She well knew that her father's study was off limits. Out of fear of disturbing him during his learning, she refrained from knocking. But her father must have heard her heavy breathing.

"Come in," she heard him say. Bashl opened the door slowly and stood respectfully in the doorway. Her father was bent over a big *gemara* engrossed in learning. When he lifted his head, he was startled by the child's flushed face and troubled eyes.

Rav Shmaryahu Yosef Karelitz

"What is it, Bashl?" he asked. "What has happened?"

She walked into the small room, which, apart from an unadorned table and chair, was furnished with a large glass-enclosed bookcase containing many old and worn *sefarim* of all sizes — Talmud, commentaries, treatises, Scripture and responsa. Her pent-up feelings of exasperation and shock rendered speech difficult. Stammering and hesitating, she began, "I heard . . . They said that you . . ."

Before she could continue, her father cut her short and, waving an admonishing finger, shouted, "*Lashon hara! Rechilus! Lashon hara!*"

Bashl's lips clamped shut. She stood frozen. The two words, *lashon hara*, and the stern and unmitigating manner in which they were uttered left a potent and indelible impression. It was a lesson never to be forgotten. Thenceforth her tongue was always on guard. It was a cardinal principle of Jewish law and ethics ingrained in her mind and heart forever that ceaseless vigilance was required in regard to one's speech. The Torah strictly forbids evil talk in all circumstances, in any shape or form, and the rabbi accordingly regarded it as his sacred duty to prevent his daughter from violating so vital a commandment. She was on the verge of transmitting an unfavorable word about someone, and it was this that her father enjoined. It was not important what the substance of the report was, who its subject was, or who authored it in the first instance. It was simply an uncompromisable wrong to state anything of an unfavorable nature about a person, any person, regardless of its veracity. That is all that mattered.

To the world at large, it doubtless would appear strange indeed that the intended victim of a slanderous comment would not care to know who had said what about him; that the impulse to strike back and retaliate, or at least defend himself, should be dormant or inhibited. But if Rav Karelitz bore any sense of outrage, it was directed not at the one who had originated the evil tale but rather at his daughter for whose conduct he was responsible. What others happened to think of him was considerably less important than the positive *mitzvah* of inculcating into his daughter traits of behavior and character in conformity with the eternal standards of his faith.

> "You shall love Hashem, your God, with all your heart, with all your soul and with all your resources. Let these matters that I command you today be upon your heart. Teach them thoroughly to your children and speak of them while you sit in your home, while you walk on the way, when you retire and when you arise."
>
> (The *Shema* Prayer; *Devarim* 6:4-9)

With constancy of purpose in thought and deed throughout his life, Rav Shmaryahu Yosef totally subordinated his will to the Master of the universe. This was the distinguishing characteristic that little Bashl sensed in her father even before she fully grasped its significance. She observed the pattern of his life, day in and day out, at close range. This was in itself a continuous, unforgettable and invaluable lesson. The transmission of the quality of virtue and righteous conduct was effectively accomplished by example and deed and not by abstract education and speech. In declaring the Jew obligated to love Hashem with all his heart and soul and might, the Torah makes it crystal clear that the commandments must be upon one's heart and soul before he or she may succeed in imparting them to his children and others. The true Jewish hero is not one who exercises dominion over others, but rather one who has complete control of himself. It was precisely this trait of self-control that was to dominate Batya's entire life.

❧ ❧ ❧

Little Bashl was inspired and guided by her revered father. With equal concern, care and intensity, her devout mother watched over

Appreciation of Life's Blessings

her every move and step and lovingly nurtured her into womanhood. The spirit which Rebbetzin Rasha Leah created and maintained within her home had far-reaching impact. This was so because she sought, first of all, to be a perfect helpmate to her husband. She sought to beautify and enhance what was already a sublime and saintly way of life. She augmented her husband's role by tackling the monumental task of raising her children and running her household with Torah wisdom and selfless love. Because she never yearned to expend her strength in vain competition with others, she never felt relegated to a position of bondage or even one of secondary importance. The daily routine of her home and family life required an expenditure of wisdom no less than the management of an empire; and in the rearing of her children, the yield could be and in fact was no less than imperial.

Devotion and sacrifice were never measured in mathematical terms, and the promotion of the common good excluded other considerations. Like the many organs of the human body, each performing its unique function while uniting and harmonizing with others to provide an effective and healthy whole, so did each member of the Karelitz family unite and harmonize with the others to build a holy and faithful house in Israel.

Life within the Karelitz household was not different in outlook from that of other Torah-observant Jewish homes at that time in Eastern Europe. These families were all steeped in the same deep-rooted traditions based upon strict and uncompromising obedience to *halachah* as an all-embracing way of life. In the management of her household and the rearing of her children, Rebbetzin Rasha Leah did, however, contribute a uniqueness of her own, a uniqueness that was telling in its lasting mark. This was a rare sense of *hakaras hatov*, an unusual recognition and appreciation of life's blessings. She sought constantly to impart this perception to her children and to impress indelibly upon them that nothing good received was ever to be taken for granted. This applied with equal validity to good given by Hashem and that bestowed by fellow humans. Any thoughtful act, trivial kindness, warm greeting, friendly smile, sigh of genuine sympathy — all these were to be promptly acknowledged with sincere and unmitigated thanks. The most deeply felt and abiding gratitude, however, was reserved for the King of Kings — for every breath of fresh air, the beauty in nature, good health, food and water, the simple comforts of home and hearth, and the all-important privilege of learning Torah.

Each day commenced with *Modeh Ani* — "I thank You." Each day ended with "Hashem is with me. I shall not fear" (*Adon Olam* prayer). Indeed this keen sense of appreciation was felt by every member of the family and never faded from morning to night. This overflowing feeling of thanksgiving was so overwhelming as to preempt opportunity in the children for bickering, petty rivalries or discord.

Perhaps, however, the most intense gratitude was felt by the rebbetzin herself. With heart and soul she gave thanks daily in her prayers for the priceless gift of precious children and for the privilege of raising them.

Children had not come easily to Rebbetzin Rasha Leah. Early in

Rebbetzin Rasha Leah Karelitz

her marriage she often fell ill, and the succession of maladies debilitated her. It seemed for a time that she would not be strong enough to bear and raise a large family, and the doctors cautioned her against having too many children, insisting that it could put her very life in jeopardy.

Rebbetzin Rasha Leah's father, Rav Shaul Katzenellenbogen, was the rav of Kossova. Shortly after her marriage, Rav Shaul relinquished his post in favor of his young son-in-law and moved to the town of Koberlin, where he was warmly received as the new spiritual leader of the Jewish community. Rav Shaul was extremely fond of his son-in-law, and he rejoiced and took pride in his distinguished academic background, his penetrating mind, and the purity of his *yiras shamayim*. Rav Shaul was immensely proud of Rasha Leah's *shidduch* and looked forward to special blessings from the union, as did his daughter.

Day and night the rebbetzin beseeched and prayed to Almighty G-d: "*Ribbono Shel Olam*, You have created me a woman. Please have mercy upon me and permit me to fulfill my calling. I wish only to fulfill my calling."

In due time the rebbetzin was blessed with nine children. With each birth her health strengthened, and she lived to the ripe-old age of ninety. The numerals nine and ninety correspond to the numerical values of *emes* — truth. Rebbetzin Rasha Leah's entire life to her last breath was dedicated to "truth and unchangeable conviction, precepts that will never fade away" (Morning prayer).

CHAPTER FOUR

Bobbe Yuspa Sets an Example

IN KOSSOVA WINTER ARRIVED EARLY and lingered late. The first snow fell in October, and thereafter it continued to fall intermittently until well into April. The accompanying cold

The King and His Servant

never allowed a thaw, even a temporary one. From the outset it was immediately evident that the dry powdery flakes were but a forerunner of more and more to come. Within an hour of the first fall the ground was a blanket of white, and destined to remain so for the ensuing six months. The countryside — forests, ancient ruins, and the old and lonely castles still inhabited by families of nobility — was covered by snow, creating a largely trackless, white spectacle of breath-taking beauty.

In town the winter scene had its special charms. The dark smoke rising from the chimneys of several hundred houses — mostly bungalows and shacks — contrasted with an equal number of snow-blanched roof tops. Were it not for the sub-zero temperature, the biting wind and the seemingly endless need to shovel and dig out, the sheer majesty of the snow would have warmed the heart. The heavy and repeated accumulations on the roads were subject to constant flattening by the traffic of horse-drawn sleighs. But the paths from homes and shops to the abutting sidewalks had to be continuously cleared to allow for movement and communication.

Layer upon layer of snow and ice grew on each side of these paths, creating vast walls.

The endless toil in the bitter cold made the Jews even more conscious of their hard life in the diaspora. The Land of Israel, their ancient homeland, with its beautiful, warm and dry spring, summer and fall seasons, seemed so far away. However, the rigors of winter were borne with quiet resignation. The Jews had followed Hashem in the desert, and they followed Him now in the cold. The climate and the place mattered little. The essence was in the following.

Nine-year-old Bashl wore almost as many stockings as there were layers of snow on the ground. All of these made it difficult to get into and then tie her high-laced shoes. Under her long winter coat she wore sweaters, and on her head a new woolen hat that matched a scarf which her older sister had recently knitted for her. The hat, which was worn low to cover the ears, was anchored in a neat bow tied under the chin. Around her neck hung a necklace-like string attached to a fur muff. Bashl completed the ensemble with a pair of warm woolen gloves and walked out to brave the weather. The moment she closed the door behind her, a sudden gust of cold wind swept a small cloud of dusty snow into her face. Instinctively she shielded herself with her scarf, leaving only the eyes exposed. She then placed her gloved hands into her muff and was off to visit her beloved paternal grandmother.

Although Bobbe Yuspa lived but a few streets away, every precaution had to be taken to protect the body from the intense cold, particularly against frostbite to a toe, finger or ear. The bundled-up Bashl, however, was perhaps more warmed by the thrill of her impending visit than by her woolen clothing. Her grandmother was lots of fun to be with. It was not that she had a playroom loaded with toys waiting for the grandchildren. Nor was there on hand a doll house with a variety of miniature furniture. In fact Bashl in all her life never owned or dressed a doll. The good times she looked forward to were of a different nature. She looked forward to all the wonderful things she was wont to learn on these visits, such as threading a needle, sewing, mending and knitting.

Rebbetzin Yuspa Karelitz

She was fascinated to observe Bobbe Yuspa take a discarded remnant of material and from it fashion tiny vests for use as undergarments by her grandchildren.

"The flannel is soft and will keep the boys warm," she would say dreamily. Then she would cut squares from the leftovers of the remnants and show Bashl how to mend or patch a worn or frayed garment.

"One should not fret about wearing patched clothes," she often said. "There certainly is nothing to be ashamed of. On the contrary, one should feel good about it — real good." And she would nod her head in earnest. "Do you know why, Bashl? Because Hashem gives us everything we have — everything. But all the wonderful things He gives us are not presents for keeps. No ... No ... Certainly not! Whatever we have is entrusted to us for safekeeping only. At any time, without warning, Hashem may take it all back. It is therefore a big, a very big sin to neglect anything Hashem Himself entrusts to us. A patch, Bashl, not only prolongs the life of a garment, but the patching demonstrates how much we appreciate everything Hashem lends us."

Bobbe handed Bashl the worn material, the patch, needle and thread. Instead of putting these to immediate use, Bashl looked up at her grandmother with eyes that had in them a blend of anticipation and hope.

"All right! All right!" Bobbe responded, smiling. "I have a story for you."

Bobbe had an inexhaustible repertoire of stories to tell, one more beautiful than the other. With one hand she picked up some knitted material to which was attached a ball of yarn and two large metallic knitting needles. With the other hand she grasped one of the needles and commenced knitting in a very mechanical manner, almost unconsciously. She paused for a moment and then began dramatically:

"Oh, what a mighty king! What a mighty king!" She shook her head wondrously from side to side as if to give credence to the description. Almost all of her stories involved a powerful potentate. Yet her reverential feeling for her subject and her simple and sincere storytelling technique never failed to imbue the story with a freshness and uniqueness, as though it were the very first story she told about the king.

"A most powerful and righteous and benevolent and wise king he was. His kingdom stretched round the entire world. Yet nothing, not even the most minute happening, ever escaped his attention. From the hidden haunts of the jungle and from the deepest ravines to the highest of mountain peaks, even where no living man had ever set foot — all these were known to the king. He of course had many servants who dutifully obeyed his orders. Some were loyal while others served begrudgingly. There were also some who were rebellious and viciously hostile. One servant, however, stood out from among them all. Yes, one servant stood out. He was not a great warrior; humble and quiet he was. He loved his king with all his heart and soul and being. For his king no hardship was too difficult and no sacrifice too great. Should the need arise, he was ready to give his very life for his king. Yes, he was ready to sacrifice his life for his king.

"The king was of course aware of this one servant's devotion. He loved him for it and protected and guided him always. At the same time the king incessantly tested the servant's loyalty. He was required to be good and obedient at all times. Yes, at all times. Once ..."

With each story Bashl's reverence for the king grew, and she came to love the king and his servant more and more. So much so that whenever the servant withstood temptation and overcame a difficult trial to which he was exposed, Bashl was thrilled. But whenever the servant succumbed to evil inclination and erred, she suffered, knowing well that the king would find it necessary to punish his beloved servant. Fortunately the ending was generally a happy one, inasmuch as the servant would sooner or later repent and be forgiven.

The stories of "The King and His Servant" were of lasting influence. So was the patching that had often accompanied the storytelling. Bashl was later to mend and patch every garment she owned. All her life, as long as there was strength in her fingers, she patched. In later years her sheets, for example, were so full of patches that there was little evidence of the original fabric.

The hour was late and Bashl readied to leave. Bobbe Yuspa hurriedly stuffed her coat pockets with goodies for the children back home. "*Pas uf!. . . Pas uf, mein kind!* (Be careful! Be careful, my child!)" she admonished Bashl with loving concern as she walked her to the door. When the door closed, Bobbe Yuspa posted herself at the window, fixing her eyes on Bashl until she was out of sight.

By the time Bashl reached home, her face had taken on a scarlet tinge from the cold, and her upper cheeks had been bitten by the wind. She removed her outer clothing quickly and stationed herself alongside the enormous, brick-faced oven in the kitchen, which served the household as both cooking appliance and space heater. Her older sister fetched a dry log, which she threw into the lively fire. Her mother then poured some essence of tea into a cup, seized the huge iron kettle steaming atop the oven, and brewed a hot cup of tea for Bashl. Meanwhile, Bashl emptied her coat pockets of the sweets Bobbe Yuspa had sent. To her dismay, she noticed that a piece of half-patched material which her grandmother had worked on had fallen out together with the sweets. With a deep and quiet sigh she picked up the material and at once asked her mother for permission to return it to her grandmother. "I took it without Bobbe's knowledge or permission," she said, obviously perturbed. Her sisters intervened and tried to persuade her not to go back into the cold.

"You did not take the patch intentionally," one of them said. "Bobbe is not a stranger. She surely will not mind. Let the matter wait till morning."

The sisters pleaded, but Bashl was not moved. Her mother was not anxious for Bashl to go out again. But in this event the fear of a possible transgression was more convincing and more cogent than the cold. The fear of Heaven had been deeply ingrained in Bashl since her infancy. The rebbetzin had always cautioned her daughters to beware of the seemingly trifling, insignificant wrongdoing, the kind committed carelessly and for which a justifiable excuse was so easy to find. She also stressed the importance of haste in the performance of a *mitzvah* and the dangers of procrastination. Accordingly, she gave Bashl permission to go. The sun was setting and indeed Bashl "made haste and did not hesitate to keep Your commandments" (*Tehillim* 119:60).

Bobbe Yuspa was overwhelmed by Bashl's unexpected return with the patch material — to be sure, not because she required or missed it, but because the incident reflected in her granddaughter traits of quality and character truly precious and rare. Like King David, she perceived that "the judgments of Hashem . . . are more desirable than gold — than even much fine gold; and sweeter than honey — than drippings from the combs" (*Tehillim* 19:10,11).

That night Bashl slept soundly. When in the morning she awoke, she found herself embellished with a new name. Her family lovingly nicknamed her "the faithful one."

IN HER YOUTH BOBBE YUSPA HAD BEEN REGARDED as one of the most beautiful girls in the district. A succession of hardships after

The Sheitel marriage, including the tragic and untimely loss of her husband, failed to mar her beauty, although she never took positive steps to preserve it. She hardly ever looked into a mirror, and when she did, it was not for the purpose of vanity but rather to ensure that she was neat and orderly and not a single hair on her head was exposed. The same hair and exceptional beauty had once caused a stir in the community and were the subject of an extraordinary story.

When she became engaged to Rav Shimshon Karelitz, the news spread fast and wide. The prefect of the district, who had ruled the peasantry with an iron hand and had continuously harassed his Jewish constituents with unjust accusations and burdensome taxes, found in the news of the engagement a useful opportunity to further oppress the Jews. On the pretext of saving an innocent and helpless bride from her "fanatic" family, he decreed that the cutting and covering of a bride's hair on the eve of her marriage amounted to inhuman cruelty, and he strictly forbade the act. Violation of the order, he announced, would subject the entire Jewish community in Kossova to heavy fines and render the officiating rabbi subject to arrest.

By depicting the Jews as a cruel people, the prefect was able to intensify the hatred of the gentiles against them. At the same time he appeared as a benevolent public official who cared only to protect and promote the welfare of his constituents. His act further provided him with an opportunity to extract from the Jews exorbitant bribes even as he enhanced his country-wide prestige at their expense. The Jewish community had long been familiar with the shenanigans of the prefect. They knew he meant business.

Had the prefect been a good-hearted man truly interested in the well-being of the young bride, he would have taken the trouble to meet with a representative of the Jewish community for an explanation of the age-old custom of covering a married woman's hair. He would have been advised that when a Jewish maiden marries, her ties to her husband are sacred. She thereafter becomes devoted solely and completely to her husband. The covering of the bride's hair symbolizes her *tznius* — modesty — and enhances the fulfillment of a commandment that seeks to demonstrate to the parties involved and to the world at large that a woman's beauty remains the private domain of husband and wife. It also affirms the Jewish view that not physical beauty but virtue and sacrifice are the ingredients that cement a Jewish marriage and make for a happy and lasting union. This theme is reiterated time and again in our holy Scriptures. Perhaps King Solomon in his *Proverbs* put best the timeless Jewish view of stressing the transcending importance of inner values as against physical appearance when he declared that "charm is deceitful and beauty vain, a woman who fears Hashem is praiseworthy" (*Mishlei* 31:30).

To the delicate and sensitive Yuspa, the decree of the prefect was a shocking and traumatic blow. The realization that the entire Jewish community could be penalized for the covering of her hair was painful. She detested and resented the prefect's unwarranted intrusion into her private affairs. She wished only to follow the ways of her mother, and that surely was not a crime!

The community prayed for mercy and a satisfactory resolution of the matter. They wondered how the rabbis would meet the decree and tackle the problem. It was not long before they were advised that the wedding would, G-d willing, take place as planned. No questions were asked. But it was clear to all that Jewish religious law would be scrupulously observed and that under no circumstances would there be a compromise of convenience.

A short but courteous letter was dispatched to the prefect informing him that the bride's own hair would be exposed for all to see as she walked to the *chupah*. An hour before the ceremony was to take place, Yuspa's long hair, neatly combed into two braids, was cut. Fortunately these two braids were sufficient to cover her entire head so that her remaining hair was not exposed. With the help of pins and the bridal headgear, the braids were neatly held in place. Thus, as far as is known to the Karelitz family, the first human-hair wig for religious purposes, the *sheitel*, came into being.

By their decision and course of action, the rabbis had no intent to deceive or outsmart anyone. Committed to the fulfillment of the commandments which their forefathers had sworn to uphold, they surely would have preferred to be left alone to guide their people unfettered and unmolested. It was not reasonable to be expected that the simple requirement that a married woman's hair be covered would be enjoined by a civil interdiction enforceable by collective punishment. But then there never was and never will be a logical rationale for the oppression of the observant Jew.

If the advent of the *sheitel* helped to stifle the attack of Torah values from without, a fresh attack was not long in coming from within. Irreligious Jews united in their thunder against the *sheitel*. They derided and abused the rabbis whom they accused of foisting the *sheitel* upon reluctant Jewish women. They concocted scornful jokes about the *sheitel* and its wearers, and thinly disguised their scorn and contempt for Orthodox practice. Many openly challenged the rabbis to "show us where in the Torah it is commanded that a married woman wear a wig." Their real purpose was simply to deride the Torah. In this respect they differed little from the prefect of Kossova. Eventually, however, the *sheitel* was rescued and elevated into a symbol of elegance, propriety and good taste, but the modern *sheitel* does not convey the message of the *sheitel* of old. On the contrary, the fashionable wig highlights precisely what Rebbetzin Yuspa's meant to hide. Few young brides know today of the pious purity that Bobbe Yuspa felt on the day she wore that first *sheitel* or the refined modesty that became part of the *tznius* which Batya Karelitz inherited.

CHAPTER FIVE

The Blessing of Contentment

EVERY THURSDAY under the personal supervision of Rav Shmaryahu Yosef, a house-to-house collection for the benefit of the town's poor and impoverished took place in Kossova.

Kavod Was Shed Every family, regardless of its own possible proximity to the poverty level, was asked to contribute what they could spare for the benefit of their less fortunate brethren. Some of these were existing on starvation diets and, though destitute, could not bring themselves to the point of begging publicly for alms. Accordingly, food of every description, including fruits and vegetables, flour, wine, eggs, preserves, dried beans, barley, and other items such as candles and firewood, were amassed and stored in an empty room behind the synagogue. The poor were invited to come freely and unnoticed on Friday morning and take what they needed so as to provide some *oneg*, some joy and holiness, to their Shabbos. This prodigious undertaking was undertaken through a desire to fulfill the commandment to love one's neighbor as oneself and to feed and otherwise provide for the poor.

Rav Shmaryahu Yosef, in his administration of the project, was careful to consider the sensitivities of both donor and donee. He insisted that full respect and gratitude be given the donor irrespective of the size of his donation. At the same time he sought assiduously to protect the confidentiality and privacy of the

40 / SILENCE IS THY PRAISE

recipient. To shame either the giver (for not giving generously enough) or the receiver could only detract from, if not utterly nullify, the great *mitzvah* to be accomplished. The public shame or humiliation of any individual, halachically equated with the spilling of blood, was to be avoided by every possible means. This was typical of the rav's constant efforts to preserve the dignity of every Jew.

Upon reaching the age of eleven, Batya assisted her father in this commendable enterprise. She helped collect the food and merchandise every week, and she maintained the cleanliness and orderliness of the storeroom. Eventually, when she was in her early teens, her father gave her full responsibility for the management of the entire project. If she appeared physically frail and petite for the job, these shortcomings were more than compensated for by a gracious heart and an alert mind. By dint of education and the example of her forebears, she had been well prepared for the position.

Late one Thursday afternoon she had completed her day's collection and carted it all to the storeroom. She carefully sorted the many items and placed everything in its proper place. She swept the floor, tidied the shelves and went to great pains to insure as far as possible that every item on display had a clean and appetizing look. When she was finished, the room resembled a showcase more than a collection center. As she was reviewing the situation and trying to decide whether or not she had neglected anything, a friend entered. She approached Batya, and in a whisper, apparently straining in an effort not to shock her, said, "I did not look to see who said it, but I heard it clearly: 'Batya works conscientiously so as to conceal the fact that she is collecting for her own benefit.' "

Batya's eyes lit up and she flushed. She paused, reflecting a moment or two, and then exclaimed, "Good! *Baruch Hashem! Baruch Hashem!*"

The rabbi's daughter, who a few years earlier had braved the cold to return a worthless piece of patch material to her grandmother, was now being accused of seeking to benefit from the poor. The true measure of Batya's mettle was in her extraordinary self-control. Her remarkable self-discipline enabled her to suppress her natural impulses. The innocent victim of a vicious slander, her normal reaction should have been anger, outrage and disgust. Nonetheless, in the face of a scurrilous attack on her integrity, she managed not only to contain her temper, but she did it without rancor, ill will or acrimony. She even succeeded in finding something positive in the slander and actually rejoiced.

Ever since taking over the collection service from her father, she had an underlying fear that the honor which accompanied her responsibilities tended to tarnish her good deed. She had been taught to run from *kavod*. When the opportunity presented itself she knew how to react. Now the aura of honor and its accompanying pride had been shed. Her good deed was whole. It was a *mitzvah* for its own sake — without the compensation of honor.

❧ ❧ ❧

IF TIME SEEMED TO PASS SLOWLY in the sleepy little country town of Kossova, it nevertheless passed profitably for the Karelitz

Hashem Knows

children. The boys studied long and difficult hours in the *beis medrash*, gaining continually in scholarship and maturity. The girls practiced *chesed* in their spare time as an avocation, earning widespread recognition and gratitude. The family as a whole became firmly established as pillars of the community. Observant Jews called them *"Die Heilige Familie."*

As the children moved from adolescence into young adulthood, it became necessary to prepare for their respective marriages. It was readily apparent that Rav Shmaryahu Yosef's meager salary would not suffice to meet the family's ever-increasing expenses. Consequently, the family made the decision to go into the yeast business.

The operation was to be conducted in the home by the women of the household. Rebbetzin Rasha Leah gave it her blessing. Appropriate public notice of the proposed venture was given, stock was purchased and trading commenced. Business developed slowly but steadily. On the days preceding a holiday, business was particularly brisk. The Jewish community bought yeast in quantity for their *yamim tovim*, and the gentiles for their festivals and holy days. Factory-made and packaged bakery products were unknown at the time. Most baking was done at home. The typical Jewish housewife baked *challah* every week for Shabbos, and many women also baked their daily bread. As for pastries, cinnamon buns and babka yeast cakes were the rage. The profits enabled the family to cover their needs, but just barely. Nevertheless, the Karelitz women were gratified by their success.

All the girls pitched in with equal ardor. Their mother's task was the bookkeeping, making sure that accounts were paid on time, maintaining the accuracy of the scale, taking *maaser* (tithes; a tenth of the profits which Jewish law obliges one to give to charity) and distributing it to the needy without delay. She constantly instructed her daughters in the halachic obligations of running a business and reproved them when they erred. Thus they received a basic training that would serve them well in later years.

Strangely enough, most of the yeast was purchased by the gentile farmers, many of whom came from distant villages. In those days Jews were prohibited by law from engaging in agriculture. The gentiles simply did not want the Jews to become attached to the land. They regarded the Jews as transients — temporary residents. This fact of life inevitably resulted in the concentration of Jews in *shtetls* and towns. Notwithstanding the demographic conditions of life and circumstance, there was always a substantial degree of commercial intercourse between Jew and gentile.

Although most of the gentile farmers were illiterate and uncouth, they did not lack common sense and cunning. They were the salt of the earth. Their proximity to the soil and their compelling need to eke out a living therefrom seemed to generate in them a practical wisdom. This was accompanied by a genuine belief that their labors to make the earth yield its produce were all for naught without the accompanying blessing of Heaven. As a result, they were basically G-d-fearing men who reverently sought

His favor. Generally they were at peace with the Jews. Only when incited by their leaders did their primitive natures surface, and then they were capable of the most horrendous acts. When not instigated to violence, however, they behaved in a proper neighborly fashion.

Consequent to the farmers' fundamental religious beliefs was their high regard for Rav Shmaryahu Yosef and his family. They were quick to perceive in the rav a man of G-d. This was especially manifest in the manner of their greeting. When passing him in the street on his way to or from the *beis medrash*, they would shout, "May the L-rd grant you a good day, Rabbi!"

Rav Shmaryahu, sometimes lost in thought, would occasionally acknowledge the greeting only belatedly. But surely no snub was intended. The farmers knew that the rav was a truly humble man and never contemplated even the slightest offense. The warm esteem in which the rav was held carried over to their patronage of his family's yeast business. They tended to view any purchase of yeast from the Karelitz family as something which was bound to impart blessing to their holiday bread. They returned again and again. They had apparently not been disappointed.

In the year 1912 soon after Succos, Rav Shmaryahu Yosef's daughter Badana became engaged to Rav Shmuel Eliyahu Kahan, a young and gifted *talmid chacham*. He was a fitting match for the virtuous daughter of the Kossova rav. The wedding was fixed for early spring, and the event became a communal one. All the Jewish women of the town came to the Karelitz home and joined Rebbetzin Rasha Leah and her five daughters in the preparatory tasks — baking, jarring preserves, pickling herring, rendering chicken fat, making feather-bed quilts, sewing the bride's wardrobe, shopping — and an endless array of other miscellaneous chores.

Preparation for a Jewish wedding was a grand enterprise and incurred great expense. To pay for it all, the rebbetzin decided to expand the stores of stock on hand and attempt to sell more yeast than ever before. Every available space in the house was cleared, scrubbed spotlessly clean and piled high with fresh merchandise.

A small shed near the railway station was rented and filled with additional merchandise. The heavy increase in inventory represented a correspondingly heavy investment, as well as an increased exposure to the perils of weather and theft. But the girls were excited by the venture. When everything was under cover and secure, they breathed a collective sigh of relief and prayed that Hashem would send them the customers so that their labors and their hopes might be crowned with success.

The best-laid plans of mortal man are subject to confirmation by a Higher authority. "Many are the thoughts in the heart of man, but the counsel of G-d endures" (*Mishlei* 19:21). And, indeed, the unexpected happened. Freakish winter-weather conditions, such as had not been experienced in living memory, suddenly set in. There was the usual heavy snow, but in addition to this, temperatures plunged. The intense cold was accompanied by winds of blizzard velocity. Powerful gusts lifted and hurled every movable object in their path, smashing them against the walls of buildings and leaving a mass of debris in their wake. The frightening situation kept almost everyone indoors. Rags were stuffed around the exterior doors and window frames to keep out the cold, while everybody huddled around the wood-burning stoves in an effort to keep warm. Children were warned to keep a distance from these stoves as well as the kerosene lamps lest they stray too close and cause a fire. The heavy frost that covered the windows, both inside and outside, added to the foreboding atmosphere.

Day after day the severe weather conditions did not relent. The Karelitz girls began to grow anxious and worried. The farmers would sooner or later obtain their yeast elsewhere. In the circumstances they could hardly be expected to make the long trip to Kossova. There was increasing apprehension that the wedding expenses would not be met. If the yeast were not sold, what would they do?

In the face of mounting concern, not a word of complaint was heard from any quarter. Rebbetzin Rasha Leah carried on, attending to her chores with her characteristic dignity. If she did occasionally sigh, it was out of concern for the elderly suffering terribly from the cold and for women in labor whose natural discomfort was seriously aggravated. She worried too about the newborn babies, and she said *Tehillim* for them.

By being essentially bound up with the plight of others, the rebbetzin had learned to maintain personal self-control in trying times. Her daughters followed her example. As they grew, they acquired a quality of serenity in the face of hardship and were largely unaffected by the vicissitudes of daily life. However, the yeast dilemma confused the girls. They became troubled and restless. They would often go to the window, scrape away the frost and seek vainly for a change in the weather.

One morning Rav Shmaryahu Yosef came into the dining room, took breakfast as usual, recited *Bircas Hamazon* with his customary deliberation, rose and started towards his study. On the way he took note of the agitation that was written on the faces of the girls. This more than disturbed him. He saw in the disquietude a lack of complete faith in the benevolence of the Almighty. He would not tolerate any such attitude. He turned to his daughters and admonished them sternly:

"We trust in Hashem at all times! He well knows our needs. Hashem knows!" With that he walked into his study and closed the door behind him.

For many hours after he had left, the impact of his words seemed to reverberate. The girls got the message. Heaven was evidently impressed as well. For that very same morning there came a sudden break in the weather. Fresh snow began to fall and the intense cold abated.

By afternoon, caravans of horse-drawn sleighs with rugged farmers aboard drove into Kossova. To the Karelitz family they appeared as heaven-sent chariots. Many made their way to the Karelitz home, calling out, "Hoy! Ahoy!" to their horses as they pulled up outside the entrance door. They came from near and far, old customers and new ones.

The scales were quickly set up in the log shed which at the beginning of winter had been loaded with firewood and was now largely empty. In a few days all of the yeast was sold, both the supplies on hand in the house and that which had been stored in the railway hut. The queue of purchasers dispersed only when the supplies had been completely exhausted.

Batya was in her teens at the time of the yeast crisis, and the miraculous events moved her deeply. Many years later she recalled them, and she never failed to be touched by their memory. Yet it was not so much the sudden spectacular arrival of the farmers and the dramatic rescue from financial ruin that had left an indelible mark. Rather, she was impressed by the eminence of those *tzaddikim* on whose behalf Hashem perennially performs miracles.

✿ ✿ ✿

Princess in Her Home

AS SARAH (a name denoting royalty) — the first of the four mothers of the Jewish people — was princess in her tent, so was Batya princess in her home. It was there that she found much of her life's satisfaction. Consequently she had no desire to holiday in faraway places. She had all she wanted in her tiny home.

Part of Batya's satisfaction was that she was moved by everything G-d given. As a result, she found a world of beauty in her kitchen. To her, every fruit or vegetable — be it beet, berry, radish or cherry — testified to the unique inventiveness, super-intelligence, and boundless generosity of the Almighty. She marveled no end:

"How great are Your deeds, Hashem; exceedingly profound are Your thoughts!" (*Tehillim* 92:6).

In appreciation, she took no food item for granted. How could anything produced by the hand of G-d be a matter of indifference? Even if it were available in plenty — an onion, a potato, for example — to Batya it was a bountiful gift of Heaven.

Batya peeling a cucumber was a picture to be seen. Her loving care and gentleness were evidenced by the thinness of the peel which fell off — so fine it was almost transparent. Her treatment of the cucumber surely reflected sensitivity to its growth. Planted in natural, rich soil, it was nourished by the sun and sold fresh only hours after it was picked. Certainly no one plucked it from its roots before it had a chance to ripen fully. It was not sprayed with glossy, sticky film, nor was it stored for months in a deep freeze and rendered lifeless like a small Egyptian mummy. It was, however, neither the freshness of the cucumber nor her poverty which induced Batya's attentive peeling. She simply detested waste. Waste she regarded as an arrogant abuse of G-d's benevolence.

Yet in later life there was a time when Batya chose to be extravagant. This was when she was married, a mother of two small sons and living in *Eretz Yisrael*.

❀　❀　❀

In 1920, the League of Nations met in Sevres, France and mandated the Land of Israel to the British. The Jews were elated. Certainly the Holy Land was better off as a British Protectorate than it had been as a Moslem-oriented, Turkish dominion. The Jews expected the British to rule lawfully, with sensitive understanding, in contrast to the behavior of the primitive, ruthless and unpredictable Turks. Unfortunately, the British takeover fell short of expectations. Dictated by self-interest, the British tended to favor the oil-rich Arabs and restricted Jewish immigration. Life in general was difficult and food was scarce. Many food items, including bread, were rationed. Another regulation — enacted with little consideration — banned the sifting of flour. The British felt that too much flour was lost in the process of sifting and that this was a luxury the impoverished population could ill afford.

For The Torah-observant community, forbidden by the Torah to consume bugs, mites or insects of any kind, bread produced under the ban was almost useless. Some observant Jews waited until their loaves of bread became semi-stale and then sliced them very thin, holding each slice to the bright sun to inspect for infestation. After removing the portions affected they were left with hardly anything edible. This situation continued for some time. Representatives of the Orthodox community protested, but the British paid no heed. The British had far more "important" things to worry about than the concerns of a small minority of Torah-observant Jews.

Batya never bought this bread. Instead she used her bread ration cards to obtain a bit of flour. It was a poor deal inasmuch as the net weight she received was far less than that of the bread she was entitled to. Upon bringing the flour home, Batya proceeded to sift it on her porch. The kitchen walls were full of cracks and she feared that flour dust might settle into them, making Pesach cleaning virtually impossible. In defiance of the ban and the outdoor breeze, she ran the flour through her sieve, not once but twice. At the end she was left with very little flour. Nevertheless she made a dough, kneaded it, watched it rise, shaped it and baked it, enjoying every moment of her labor.

To Batya, quantity was not important. She rejoiced in her portion regardless of its size. By the same token, she knew well that her undersized lot could be richly blessed even as a gift of plenty could be blighted. It all depended on doing what was proper in the eyes of Hashem.

☙ ☙ ☙

THE FOCAL POINT IN BATYA'S PARENTS' home was the dining room. It contained a long table about forty inches in width.

The Altar Surrounding the table were twelve or more chairs. The table and chairs were the most-used furniture in the house. All meals were served on this table — those of Shabbos, *Yom Tov* and weekdays as well. At this table the frequent visitors to the Karelitz home were entertained, served tea with lump sugar, cookies and *lekach* (sponge cake). The table was also used for Torah study, especially late at night and even into the morning hours. The chairs, wooden and without upholstery, were a distinct aid against drowsiness and conducive to mental alertness.

Since the destruction of the *Beis Hamikdash*, the dining-room table has traditionally served as a substitute for the *mizbei'ach*, the Temple Altar. Accordingly, in the Karelitz household all meals were taken in a reverent, correct and respectful attitude. Table manners were never relaxed. Hands were always washed before a meal, and the fore blessings and after blessings were recited. Food and drink were always taken seated. It was unthinkable to move about the room while eating.

At every meal, either a family member or guest would deliver a point of *halachah*, a thought on the portion of the week or a *mussar vort*. Often it would trigger an animated discussion. Mealtime thus became an uplifting and spiritual experience.

On Shabbos and *Yom Tov* the table was graced with an immaculate, white tablecloth and cheerfully illuminated by burning candles in silver candlesticks. These were surrounded by a decanter of wine, *challah* and a variety of delicacies.

From childhood on, Batya was fascinated by the spiritual aura of the dining-room table. Early in life she matured sufficiently to supervise its use. The awareness that it was in her power to transform an ordinary wooden table into a holy altar enthralled her. All her life she devoted herself to the sanctification of the table and by doing so converted her modest home, wherever it was, into a small sanctuary. This obsession, however, never led her to neglect other *mitzvos*. On the contrary, Batya's whole sensibility, her whole being, lived the truism that as G-d is One, so is His Torah indivisible. She devoted herself wholly to every *mitzvah* within her competence and ability to perform; and as she achieved mastery of those she had undertaken, she ventured to fulfill others, as it is written: "One *mitzvah* begets another *mitzvah*" (*Pirkei Avos* 4:2).

Thanks to the spirit of Torah learning that pervaded her home, Batya possessed a conceptual approach to everything about her. She regarded, for example, the Sanctuary, including the Altar, as a reflection of the order of creation. Her first priority in every undertaking was therefore order and purpose, for this was the way of Hashem. No feature of her home could be outside the framework of order and purpose. Thus the tablecloth she used was more than a mere cover concealing an old and worn table. Nor did the tablecloth represent elegance for the sake of elegance. That was not the way of Hashem. The concept of covering bareness has permeated the thinking of man since creation. It is particularly ingrained in the Jewish psyche. To Batya, the tablecloth was a symbol of dignity and respect. The Almighty had covered the earth with adorning and nourishing vegetation and transformed bareness into glory. So did Batya seek to impart to the plain table in her dining room something of the reverence of the Altar. She prayed that her efforts be deserving of this desired end.

As to the preparation and consumption of food, Batya conformed to the highest religious standards. She knew that Torah directed not only the practice of an ideal life, but prescribed in detail the dietary rules to sustain it. Calorie counts, synthetic vitamins and fiber content were to her irrelevant, and she gave no thought to them. *Kashrus* was her prime criterion in the preparation of wholesome and good-tasting dishes. She regarded the mind as the ultimate objective of nourishment, because the mind was the instrument of Torah study, the pre-eminent activity of the Jew. For this reason she did not yield to the blandishments of piquant delights that rouse the appetite and increase one's craving of gourmet pleasures. Her dishes more closely approximated the taste of manna, the food which Hashem rained down on the Israelites in the desert, and the effect was much the same. Small portions sufficed, but the delicious taste lingered on and satisfied.

Aesthetics too played a role. Batya would set the table in beautiful fashion and serve the meals with appropriate style. Again this was not the product of whim or caprice. Hashem did not deck out the world haphazardly. He "clothed it in majesty" (*Tehillim* 104:1). So too did Batya make sure that the altar was embellished fittingly. Even the floor beneath the table was not unattended. It was maintained immaculately. It never bore traces of food between meals. It was deemed almost sacrilegious to trod on bread or *challah* crumbs.

When the meal was cooked, the table set and dinner ready to be served, Batya was in no rush to sit down. Like the ancient *Kohanim*, she first checked her person. She removed her apron and examined her dress for possible stains. Before the ritual washing of her hands, she would scrub them and check her fingernails. They were always kept short and neat and clean.

When at last she seated herself at the table, however hungry she may have been, she never shed her composure or her manners. She ate slowly and in a refined manner. She remembered always that she was at the altar. Eating was more than a biological process. A meal was in the nature of an offering and a thanksgiving feast. It was a sacred act to which *kedushah*, holiness, had been imparted.

When the meal was ended, Batya would wash her hands anew, with the same self-control as at the start, meditate on G-d's graces and say *Bircas Hamazon*: "Blessed are You, Hashem, our G-d, King of the universe, Who nourishes the entire world, in His goodness — with grace, with kindness and with mercy ..."

CHAPTER SIX
The Struggle Within

SINCE THE DESTRUCTION of the Second Temple, two continuous calamities have afflicted the Jewish people: dispersion and anti-Semitism. In his merciful Divine Providence, Hashem

The Four Brothers designed the second malady to counteract the ravages of the first. Historically, anti-Semitism prevented the Jewish people from assimilating with their tormentors. Persecution shielded the Jew from the influence of strange cultures. Indeed the more scattered and disliked the Jews were, the more guarded was their solidarity and their uniqueness.

Ironically when a measure of freedom and equality was granted to the Jewish people, it threatened this solidarity. The rise of all the "isms" during the last three centuries — Jewish Rationalism known as the *Haskalah* movement, Reform Judaism, Marxism, Communism, Socialism, Zionism — split the Jewish nation into fragments. As a result, Jews abandoned their faith in droves.

In the course of time, disputes flared up among the Torah-observant leadership regarding how best to counter these inroads upon Torah observance. Some advocated leniency and tolerance toward the misguided deserters and rebels. This course encouraged compromise and more often than not, merely slowed the course of assimilation. Others insisted on strict unbending Torah observance, for they foresaw the consequences of encouraging those who advocated rebellion against the Torah.

In these tumultuous times a ray of sunshine emanated from Kossova to brighten the Jewish world scene. This was due in large measure to the family of Batya Karelitz and the particular talents and virtues of each of its members. Above and beyond their individual contributions, they shared a zeal for the practice, teaching and transmission of unyielding, Torah-true *Yiddishkeit*. Their lives were imbued with understanding and compassion for their fellow Jews while resisting firmly and uncompromisingly the various assaults upon their faith. They practiced and fostered a blend of strict loyalty to Torah values with a tender benevolence and warmth in their relations with fellow Jews. This rare combination of virtues was later to be of enormous value to Jewish religious growth. Indeed, the legacy inherited from the Karelitz family remains crucial to the stability of the Torah community in our own time.

In the face of the impending dangers, all four of Batya's brothers braced to fight the enemy that threatened Jewish religious life from within. All four were mild mannered by nature. None was a warrior at heart. Nevertheless, they were totally and selflessly dedicated to the defense of Torah and ready to counter the assaults on their faith on all fronts.

The leading protagonist was Batya's oldest brother, Rav Meir Karelitz. Some time after he married his wife Miriam, his distinguished father-in-law, Rav Shlomo Cohen, urged him to move from rural Kossova to Vilna and share the pulpit with him. Vilna at that time was hailed as the "Yerushalayim of the Diaspora" — the international center of Torah study. Rav Meir welcomed the proposal. He considered the opportunity of being surrounded by eminent Torah scholars — studying under and with them and serving them in this hour of need — a privilege and duty. Without hesitation he accepted the offer and transferred to Vilna.

In Vilna, sharing the pulpit of his father-in-law, Rav Meir spoke out vigorously and inspiringly, urging his audiences neither to

Rabbi Meir Karelitz

forget nor forfeit their eternal heritage. In addition, he founded a yeshivah catering especially to bright and gifted pupils. The times were such that the *masmidim*, the most diligent and studious, needed particular protection and encouragement. They were prime targets of ideologues who aimed to confuse and brainwash them. The *Haskalah* movement, calling itself "Enlightenment," tried to create a new Jewish culture, melding portions of the Torah that suited them with the "modern" advances of European civilization. Its exponents, the *Maskilim*, mocked Torah sages, hoping to induce yeshivah boys to abandon the arduous task of learning Torah. Torah was their most formidable foe. They fought ruthlessly against the letter and spirit of Torah, their favorite weapon being derision. As a result, many of the tender young were torn by conflicting influences. Bewildered, they did not know which path to take.

Rav Meir fought back. His most effective weapon was Torah truth. With it he kindled in the hearts of his *talmidim* a light —

bright and everlasting. To Rav Meir nothing was more important than saving these precious Jewish seedlings for Torah study.

This was not the sole cause that he championed. Protecting the integrity of the Torah sages was another battle that he waged. There was a desperate need to fight off the ceaseless assaults to which the sages were exposed. The Chafetz Chaim and Rav Chaim Ozer Grodzenski were among the most prominent Torah giants of their time. As such, they were constantly subjected to vile public attacks by the secularists. The affront pained and alarmed Rav Meir. He resolved to protect them with every means at his disposal.

In 1915, even before the Communists had consolidated their power on Russian soil, they attacked and destroyed religious institutions, even threatening the famous yeshivah at Radin and the lives of its *rebbai'im* and *talmidim*. Their revered dean, the Chafetz Chaim, dispatched an urgent plea for help to Rav Chaim Ozer. Rav Meir Karelitz, along with his most gifted *talmid* and future brother-in-law, Rav Shmuel Greineman, was placed in charge of the daring rescue operation. Risking his life, he traveled to Radin, quickly assembled the students and managed to smuggle them out in the nick of time.

Batya's second-oldest brother, Rav Avraham Yeshayahu (the Chazon Ish), was one of the leading Talmudic scholars of his time. He possessed a keen and perceptive mind and was blessed with an extrasensory vision which enabled him to recognize and understand the role of the Jew. He accordingly shunned the limelight and sought only to fulfill the will of Hashem.

Early in life Reb Avraham Yeshayahu was drawn magnetically to the ancient and mysterious pages of the Talmud. The writing fascinated him and he dug deeply into its content. The deeper he dug, the more treasures he discovered. With each find his hunger grew until his whole life became one long, dedicated treasure hunt. He was totally consumed by the wisdom and depth of the Talmud, and he studied it with superhuman intensity and diligence. He explained his motivation: "When we study the

The Chazon Ish

Talmud, it is Hashem Who speaks to us." He listened carefully to its every word.

The more his spirituality soared, the more humble he became. Earthly comfort had not the slightest attraction for him. Only to come closer and closer to his Master was his life's ambition. On this he commented: "Nothing in life ever gave me more pleasure than doing the will of Hashem." What that will was he well knew.

Rav Avraham Yeshayahu acquired enormous scientific know-how, which he utilized to the utmost. His lone source was *Chazal*. He chose to learn medicine from the Healer of the sick, astronomy from the Creator of heaven, law from the Supreme Judge, and longevity from the Eternal One. The proofs of his proficiency were the many well-known physicians and surgeons who frequently consulted him on medical procedure and heeded his advice. A broad spectrum of questions on astronomy, biology and the sciences relating to *halachah* found their way to his door as well.

By the time Rav Avraham Yeshayahu was eligible for marriage, his potential as a major figure in the Torah world was well recognized. Yet he made clear to his future wife, Batya (the same name as his sister), in a meeting before their marriage, that he had no intention of becoming either a rav or a *rosh yeshivah*. His only wish was to devote his life to study, prayer and writing. Batya was impressed by his integrity and his selfless devotion to Hashem. There were always, however, some who found fault with a young man who did nothing but "sit and learn." Selfless devotion to Hashem has often been misconstrued by those incapable of such sacrifice.

In 1911, eleven years after his marriage, Rav Avraham Yeshayahu published his first work. He adopted the pen name Chazon Ish* in the hope it would shield him from the public eye. Torah scholars, however, searched for clues that would reveal the undisclosed author. By the time his seventh volume of works appeared, there were few within the Torah world who did not know his identity. Ironically, the name that was supposed to hide his identity became the name by which he was soon to be world renowned. Indeed, the name became so beloved that even near kin referred to him as the Chazon Ish. Moreover, the prominence attached to the name reflected upon every member of the family. It added luster to the Karelitz name for generations to come. Rebbetzin Batya was often referred to as the "sister of the Chazon Ish."

In time, the Chazon Ish became widely recognized as the *gadol hador* (leader of the generation). As such, he assumed the sacred obligation to rescue his people from the hands of the perplexed, the indifferent and the scornful. He knew his enemies well. They were not unlike the enemies of old. In other guises, they had all surfaced

---

* *Chazon Ish* in Hebrew means "vision of a man." *Ish* is also an acronym of the name Avraham Yeshayahu.

Rav Yitzchok Zundel

before. Because the Chazon Ish knew his adversaries and was equipped with the perceptive vision to deal with them successfully, he was undaunted by the overwhelming odds he faced. In a quiet way, hidden from the eyes of the world, he inspired and nurtured a small settlement in the Holy Land known as Bnei Brak. To it, he transmitted much of his enormous spiritual wealth. From there, rays of Torah radiated the world over to nourish observant Jews.

The family of Batya Karelitz was homogeneous. Even those members who joined the family through marriage were as though born into it. This of course did not detract from the unique individuality of each family member. Thus Batya's third brother, Rav Yitzchok Zundel, was perhaps the most saintly. His concentrated learning so purified his soul that he became the epitome of *tzidkus* — righteousness. His very appearance had an angelic quality. Jew and gentile, the celebrated and the ordinary, spoke of him with reverence. He had no need to preach or demonstrate his

Rabbi Moshe Karelitz

convictions. His very being testified to the fact that man is created in the image of G-d. The fight against all the "isms" was a spiritual one. Rav Yitzchok Zundel's secret weapon lay in simply being an exemplary Jew who looked only to "find favor and good understanding in the eyes of Hashem and man" (*Mishlei* 3:4). Everybody loved him — everybody, that is, except the Germans.

Batya's fourth brother, Rav Moshe Karelitz, was motivated in the main by a tender attachment to his fellow Jew. Like his oldest brother, Rav Meir, he left Kossova soon after he married and settled on the outskirts of Vilna. There he officiated as rabbi. Again like Rav Meir, he was surrounded by gifted young students who were devoted to him heart and soul. Rav Moshe enriched them with a burning love for Torah.

Rav Moshe's principal organ of influence was the monthly journal *Knesset Yisrael*, which he edited and published. It contained Talmudic expositions written by well-known Talmudic scholars. From time to time he included articles of his own, which largely reflected his commitment to the teachings of the Chafetz Chaim and Rav Chaim Ozer.

Though he was involved in a wide range of activities, Rav Moshe was nevertheless poor — perhaps the poorest Karelitz of all. Yet few were aware of his deprivation, because poverty had little relevance to his way of life. He was happy with his lot. Nothing seemed to be missing. There was one earthly possession, however, to which Rav Moshe attached importance. This was an elegant overcoat which he had been given on his wedding day. It was no mere sentimentality that caused him to take care of this coat in such a manner that neither time nor wear and tear could affect its condition. His purpose was neither to hide his tattered suits nor to impress anyone. He simply wished to pay his respect to others. His coat enabled him to dress as if he were about to visit important dignitaries. To him, each and every fellow Jew was worthy of this special homage and deserving of this esteem.

❀ ❀ ❀

Each of the brothers in his own way made a potent and indelible mark. The dedicated activism of Rav Meir, the halachic leadership of the Chazon Ish, the spirituality of Rav Yitzchok Zundel and the warmth and zeal of Rav Moshe combined to enhance, promote and strengthen the honor of Torah at a time when much of world Jewry was looking in the wrong direction for inspiration.

CHAPTER SEVEN
War and Peace, Danger and Rescue, Sorrow and Joy

IT WAS THE CALM BEFORE THE STORM immediately before World War I. The ordinary folk would never have dared to predict or even imagine that Europe stood on the threshold of cataclysm. Many within the Karelitz family consid-

Wildfire ered the time ideal to find Batya a suitable match. Two of her older sisters had married and the third was engaged. Now it was her turn. Her brothers were on the lookout for possible candidates. Their close contact with many young and gifted yeshivah students enabled them to evaluate, distinguish and assess their background, character and worthiness. The Chazon Ish had recommended Rav Shmuel Eliyahu Kahan for his sister Badana. Rav Meir Karelitz had promoted his best *talmid*, Rav Shmuel Greineman, for his sister Tzivia. Only Rav Abba Swiatycki, who was married to Enya Chaya, had managed to find his way into the family independent of the brothers. He nevertheless fit in very well and the brothers were extremely fond of him.

In spite of the desirable contacts the brothers enjoyed, it was not easy to find a suitable young man for Batya. Indeed, they had difficulty in finding a match worthy of her. Batya waited patiently. She trusted Hashem, knowing well that in due time she would get what she was meant to have.

The search was underway when in August 1914 — on *Tishah B'Av* in the Jewish year of 5674 — war erupted in Europe. In Hebrew, 5674 is תרע"ד, which also means *will tremble*. Indeed, the shocked world trembled mightily. It was as if fire had suddenly burst forth. This wildfire spread from the city of Berlin, the cradle of "enlightened Rationalism." It was from this hotbed of liberalism that the deadly fumes burst forth. The same Germans, who spawned the most brilliant thinkers and whose psychiatrists had dug deep into the innermost sanctum of the subconscious, embarked upon a purposeless and devastating war that spread crazily until it engulfed virtually the entire civilized world.

In the big cities the ordeal resulting from the German onslaught, occupation and subsequent retreat was particularly horrible. In Vilna, for example, the scarcity of food was so acute that thousands died of starvation. Countless corpses — dead infants, children and the elderly — lay strewn about the streets. The few emaciated men who had not been mobilized into the army did not have strength to cope with burials.

It was miraculous that Kossova was spared from devastation by both the Germans and the Russians. The town, however, was just as famine stricken as the rest of war-torn Europe.

Batya's duties included managing the kitchen. Her training in thrift came in handy. Her sisters, of course, helped but she was more or less in control because she seemed to be able to improvise meals from thin air. Her family had long been accustomed to a lean and meager level of subsistence. The hunger pangs were therefore not as acutely felt as they may have been otherwise.

The dire circumstances compelled Batya to ration the food she prepared. Each member of the family received an equal portion and made the best of the situation. Only Batya's oldest brother-in-law, Rav Abba Swiatycki, complicated matters. Every morning he would come for his allotted portion and disappear. A few hours later he would revisit the kitchen and ask his rebbetzin: "Can you spare something for me, Enya Chaya?" There was painful distress in his voice. The devoted wife said not a word. There was no point in trying to refresh her husband's memory. He was known to have had an excellent one. Rav Abba, on the other hand, sensed that an explanation was in order. He would add, "I don't know why, but my heart is unusually weak today; it pains me terribly."

Rebbetzin Enya Chaya reexamined the family's dwindling supply of food. She counted and recounted, weighed and reweighed. Then she handed her husband more than she could spare, because she knew that he invariably gave his small portion to some starving child. What he himself lived on was a mystery.

Near the end of the war Rav Shmaryahu Yosef fell ill. His condition worsened gradually. He lacked the strength to pull through the war years. To Batya the most tragic chapter of World War I was her father's difficult illness and the painful end that ensued. Somehow she could not visualize her little world without her father's dignified presence and invaluable counsel.

The people of Kossova shared Batya's feelings. Even the gentile farmers were distressed by the rav's ill health. Not that they lacked troubles of their own. As always, they had been exploited and plundered by various invading armies. But their respect for the rabbi of Kossova was real and sincere. They came from time to time to the Karelitz home to inquire as to his well-being. Before departing they often left a little bundle they had hidden under their sheepskin coats. A gift of potato peels, a few eggs or other such precious food was indeed much appreciated. It certainly was generous of them to remember the rabbi's family at a time when they too felt the pinch of famine.

In spite of the hazardous rail and road conditions then prevailing, Rav Meir Karelitz braved the trip from Vilna to Kossova to pay his sick father a heartwarming visit. All went well until he was on his way back to Vilna. In one of the small villages en route home, he was apprehended and spuriously charged with espionage. The local rabbi intervened, and Rav Meir was placed under house arrest. When the news of Rav Shmaryahu Yosef's passing reached him, he was still confined. He pleaded with the authorities to allow him to attend his father's funeral but they refused. In the midst of the ongoing military crisis, the simple desire to attend an old father's funeral was viewed as outrageous and treasonous.

Soon thereafter the war ended. Rav Meir was released and he made his way back home to Vilna. Almost immediately after his arrival he was entrusted with the complicated rescue operations of yeshivah students who were threatened by the Bolsheviks. There were two phases to the undertaking — both hazardous: the speedy extrication of the boys from Communist hands and the need to smuggle them into Poland or Lithuania. Neither was an easy task, inasmuch as the authorities refused to grant entry permits to Jews. Upon entering Polish or Lithuanian soil the students had to be dispersed and hidden at great risk, lest their discovery lead to prompt deportation. Political asylum did not apply to Jews.

Among the many young men who found shelter in Rav Meir's home was the scholarly Rav Nochum Meir Zibolnik. After giving the matter some thought, Rav Meir decided to send this gifted young man to Kossova. This was more easily decided than accomplished. Rav Nochum Meir lacked the identification papers needed for travel. There was no free movement in the early 1920's in most of Europe. People were continuously searched and molested on the streets, roads and trains by suspicious police on the lookout for illegal aliens. Proper identification was of paramount importance. Rav Meir was, nevertheless, unperturbed. He simply prefaced the name Nochum to his own identification papers so that they read: Nochum Meir Karelitz. After examining the change carefully, he concluded that the documents were worthy of use. Handing them to Rav Zibolnik he said: "From now on you shall be known as Nochum Meir Karelitz. With the help of Hashem these papers should enable you to reach Kossova without difficulty. I am hopeful that the facilities for learning there will be to your liking. My family will surely make you feel at home."

Not only did Rav Nochum Meir adopt the family name for life, but his coming to Kossova resulted in a union that lasted as long. Soon after his arrival in Kossova he became the celebrated groom of Batya Karelitz.

It is well known that Hashem pairs couples according to merit.

Rav Nochum Meir

Seldom were two people more perfectly matched or more deserving of each other. The union was living testimony of the fact that marriages are made in Heaven. Their similar natures suggested that both *chasan* and *kallah* had enjoyed the same kind of upbringing, even though Batya had been raised by her loving parents in a sheltered home while Rav Nochum Meir was orphaned in infancy. Indeed, bitterness and loneliness were not part of Rav Nochum Meir's disposition because he had the good fortune of having been raised in the home of his maternal uncle, Rav Shlomo Golovanchitz.

The Golovanchitz family was well known in Lithuanian Torah circles. As a Talmudic scholar, lecturer and spiritual leader in the Mohinor and Mohilo villages, Rav Shlomo possessed both the wisdom and compassion needed to raise his sister's orphaned child.

Indeed, his profound influence was noted in Rav Nochum Meir's rare devotion to the Creator and His Torah, as well as in his dignified, soft-spoken manner. Most indicative of Rav Shlomo's influence in the rearing of his orphaned nephew, however, was Rav Nochum Meir's passionate love for children. For indeed how could an orphan develop so unusual a feeling for children unless he himself had experienced that same kind of affection in the tender years of his youth? The adult tends to impart to children only that which was instilled in him during his own childhood years. This was movingly demonstrated years later when Rav Nochum Meir resided in *Eretz Yisrael*, the father of two sons.

❧ ❧ ❧

During the British mandate of Palestine there was an outbreak of typhoid fever in the Middle East. Isolated cases occurred in the Land of Israel. One child on Rav Nochum Meir's street was stricken. The news spread with lightning speed. Panic-stricken mothers grabbed their children and sped away as fast and as far as they could from the area of contagion. Rav Nochum Meir was on his way as well, but in the opposite direction. He had known the sick little boy by sight and very much wished to make a friendly sick call. The quarantined parents were dumbfounded when they beheld Rav Nochum Meir on their doorstep.

Rav Nochum Meir put the worried parents at ease. He explained that the Talmud teaches one how to deal with contagious diseases, and he made nothing of the dangers to himself. Indeed, the faith Rav Nochum Meir thus generated had a tranquilizing and therapeutic effect on all the parties involved. In difficult times there is nothing more pacifying than the beneficial addiction to faith. Furthermore, the commandment to visit the sick in itself provides a useful remedy. Rav Nochum Meir's visit would relax the child and thus help relieve the malady. At the same time the merit of the good deed immunized Rav Nochum Meir against the disease.

Rav Nochum Meir's fervent wish was to lighten the child's ailment so that he gain strength to fight the disease. He visited him again and again. Once he found himself in the little boy's company he gave him his all. He played with him and related stories until a sweet smile appeared on the child's face. The scene was touching.

With the help of Hashem the child eventually recovered. The grateful parents did not quickly forget Rav Nochum Meir's contribution. Most amazing to them, however, was the gentle and patient concern the rabbi had shown their son.

How did this man develop such gentleness and understanding? Many wondered. Obviously the parents were not aware of Rav Nochum Meir's unique upbringing and the very important role his uncle, Rav Shlomo Golovanchitz, had played. Rav Shlomo himself never knew the extent of his contribution in the difficult task of finding a suitable marriage partner for Batya.

❈   ❈   ❈

One Gold Ring

WHEN THE SMOKE AND DUST OF WORLD WAR I had settled, the bleak mood of the populace resembled the shambles of the countryside. The measure of the war's senselessness was fully evident only when it was all over. Perhaps in all history there had not been a more purposeless war. Yet there were few who realized that four years of warfare on a scale theretofore unknown had simply been the punishment meted out by Hashem in response to national and individual transgression. Likewise, too few realized that the aftereffects were to continue long after the signing of the peace treaty of Versailles. Perhaps the most regrettable event resulting from World War I was the toleration at its conclusion of the Communist infection. Viewed from hindsight, allowing Communism a foothold in Russia was a tragic and enduring blunder.

The Communists moved cunningly. Even before the free world had settled down to eulogizing its dead and embarking upon the arduous task of reconstruction, their bloodletting commenced in earnest. By that time, the world was too tired to intervene. It was easier and more convenient to wash one's hands clean of the

Russian mess and to regard the revolution as an internal Russian affair.

In contrast to the bad news coming out of Russia, a powerful feeling of genuine hope for a better future was taking hold in the free world. There was optimism that a better world was in the making. Never again would there be warring among the nations. This was the setting in which Batya's wedding day took place.

As always when one of Rebbetzin Rasha Leah's children was about to marry, all of the townspeople became involved in the preparations. Batya was of course appreciative of all the kindnesses shown her, but she was determined to take full charge of the necessary arrangements herself. She went to great pains to personally oversee every last detail. Her wedding clothes and trousseau had to reflect her taste and conform to her standards. At the same time, she was extremely careful not to offend anyone. If her resolve was firm, her demeanor was gentle. In any event, it was not her personal will that was important. Above all, she wished only to carry out the will of G-d and to please Him.

Notable in her preparations for the wedding was the avoidance of any possible excess. Batya was constantly alert to the danger of waste, knowing well the tendency to be extravagant and overindulge on joyous occasions. Poverty alone was insufficient to protect against this inclination. In this respect Satan often succeeded in tempting even the pious poor, and Batya was determined not to fall into the trap. Indeed it took much self-control and wisdom to attain a proper balance between generosity and avoidance of waste.

Batya looked forward to devoting time and energy to the preparation of her wardrobe. While aware of a bride's privilege to be selective and wishing to appear as elegant as brides were wont to be, she nevertheless avoided flashy styles. She concentrated instead on outfits that were smart, trim and functional. She carefully scrutinized the fabrics to be used in the sewing. Red, pink or purple in any color scheme rendered the material distasteful to her. Only the most subdued and refined textiles were acceptable. The styles she chose were uniformly simple. Her dresses never went out of fashion. The sleeves covered the wrist, the neck line was closed, and the skirt length was a drop above the ankles. No gown was allowed to fit too snugly or to be excessively baggy. The accent was always on normality and good taste. Therein lay the beauty.

Batya's wardrobe ultimately consisted of several Shabbos and holiday dresses, one smart blouse and skirt combination for Rosh Chodesh, and a dressy, snow-white blouse and skirt ensemble for Rosh Hashanah and Yom Kippur. Although the air of newness was all about her, Batya was not quick to discard her old outfits. She neither tired of the outmoded nor became overly excited with the fashionable. The wearability of the attire and the purpose it served were all that mattered. Accordingly, she mended and patched every usable garment.

Regardless of what she wore, new or old, her sweetness and dignity shone through. Every outfit seemed to compliment her inner light. This was so because her guarded speech and unassuming modesty were so appealing that one scarcely noticed what she wore.

One chore that Batya was spared was the task of preparing the list of guests and the seating arrangements. Lest anyone's feelings be hurt for lack of an invitation, all of Kossova was invited to the wedding.

The *chupah* was held on the grounds of the synagogue. Escorted by her mother, Batya walked from her home to the canopy, where Rav Nochum Meir stood waiting. A throng of friends and well-wishers followed her.

The inner joy felt by all present was genuine. All hearts filled with good wishes for the *chasan* and *kallah*. At the same time there was an awareness of the absence of Rav Shmaryahu Yosef. No one doubted, however, that he was present in spirit and that he was surely proud of the scene that presented itself. Within and around the *chupah* stood a contingent of Jewish royalty. The bride's four brothers — Rav Meir, the Chazon Ish, Rav Yitzchak Zundel and Rav Moshe — were already distinguished personalities, each in his own right. Her brothers-in-law were no less royal.

Only Miriam, Batya's youngest sister, was still single. She was soon to marry Rav Yaakov Yisroel Kanievsky, who later became world renowned as the Steipler Gaon. The family portrait was indeed impressive and none got a better view of the proceedings than Rav Shmaryahu Yosef from his perspective on high.

During the ceremony the assembled listened solemnly as Rav Nochum Meir pronounced slowly and deliberately, "You are consecrated unto me with this ring according to the Laws of Moses and Israel." These simple words had perhaps never rung more true, never had more meaning. The intensity and deep-felt sincerity of the words were heightened by the awareness that this one gold ring which Rav Nochum Meir placed upon Batya's finger was all the wealth that he possessed. His miraculous escape from the claws of the Russian Bolsheviks had left him penniless — without even his family name. But then Rav Nochum Meir knew that he required no more than a single gold ring to consecrate his union with Batya. It brought him a life of "peace and tranquility, a meaningful life wherein Hashem delighteth" (*Shabbos Minchah* prayer).

CHAPTER EIGHT
Devotion Is the Spice of Life

THE JEWISH INHABITANTS OF KOSSOVA did not return
to their normal, everyday routine until the newlyweds had
celebrated the last of the *sheva brachos*. Every day, for seven days,

A Time for
Miracles
blessings were bestowed upon the young couple
by relatives and friends. All of Kossova joined in
the spirit of well-wishing. As soon as the
celebrations were over, however, Rav Nochum Meir returned to
his *sefarim*, and Rebbetzin Batya rejoiced in her housekeeping
chores and caring for the needs of her husband. Learning Torah
and living in accordance with its commandments were the axis
upon which their lives revolved. Each partner greatly appreciated
and valued the other's role in this mutual effort. The more the
rebbetzin tried to please her husband, the more intensively he was
able to learn. She in turn sensed a growing share in his
achievements.

❀   ❀   ❀

One beautiful summer day Rav Nochum Meir closed his books
and took his rebbetzin on an outing to the big city of Vilna. They
looked forward to visiting the many members of their families
who lived in and about Vilna. Most of all they longed to be
entertained by their many nephews and nieces, who must have

grown considerably since they had last seen them. There was a visible change in Rebbetzin Batya's appearance as well. She was in the advanced stages of her first pregnancy.

After a pleasant and uneventful trip, they arrived in Vilna. Upon knocking on the many familiar doors, they were disappointed to learn that none of their relatives were at home. It seemed that everybody had taken advantage of the unusually warm weather and gone to enjoy the beautiful woodlands nearby.

While Rav Nochum Meir and his wife were considering their next move, the baby suddenly decided to make its own move. In fact, the baby was quite resolute and persistent about the matter. At the time there were of course no private telephones or readily available transportation to enable one to call for help or reach help. Ignoring the dilemma and the extreme difficulty of the situation, the baby was born right then and there.

The *bris milah* was celebrated on time and the proud parents fittingly named their first-born son Shmaryahu Yosef, after his maternal grandfather. Additionally, in a desire to give special thanks to Hashem, Rebbetzin Batya wished to record the miraculous nature of the event. She therefore added the name Nissim, which, literally translated, means "miracles." In time the child was to become known as Nissim Karelitz and eventually as Reb Nissim.

Upon holding the baby in her arms for the first time, Rebbetzin Batya placed a small, white skullcap on his tiny head. She had sewn it herself and carried it with her wherever she went just in case she was to give birth to a little boy. The custom-made skullcap fit perfectly. From the glow in her eyes, it was apparent that she admired the child's Jewish look. But why attach such significance to a small skullcap?

The answer was evident in its Hebrew equivalent, *yarmulke,* which is a combination of two words, *yarei me'Eloka,* meaning, "One who fears Hashem."

But why the rush? Why was it necessary to start so early?

"The beginning of wisdom is the fear of the L-rd" (*Tehillim* 111:10). For Rebbetzin Batya that beginning was never too soon.

Just as she fussed with her baby's physical needs and provided him with a mother's warm and tender loving care and protection, she endeavored to be watchful as well of his soul. Long before the child reached the age of understanding, she wished the *yarmulke* to carry the message that Hashem was ever above. This recognition was to grow with the child in his subconscious awareness. The skullcap also served to cover and shield a head that would in later years house a phenomenal knowledge of Torah.

Interestingly it was little Nissim's future father-in-law, Rav Zvi Kopfshitz, whose surname incidentally means skullcap in Yiddish, who was once asked by a group of women when a child's education begins. They were familiar with the admonition that sons should be brought up as "cultivated plants" (*Tehillim* 144:12) and not as wild growth that sprouts without care and supervision. But they wanted Rav Kopfshitz to pinpoint the time. He considered the question one of the utmost importance and carefully worded his answer. "A child's rearing," he said solemnly, "does not start at the age of three, when he begins to learn the *aleph-beis*; nor does it begin at the time of his birth. It actually begins the day his mother is born. The background of the mother is crucial." Obviously little Nissim was fortunate to have been blessed with a fine beginning.

Rebbetzin Batya's second child was due in midwinter. This time she did not leave her immediate surroundings for the duration of the pregnancy. She generally remained close to home and hardly ever ventured outdoors.

Like everyone else at Chanukah time the Karelitz's cleared the frost from the one window that faced the street in order to allow the illuminated *menorah* to advertise the miraculous days of old. After Rav Nochum Meir had performed the lighting ceremony, the rebbetzin yielded to the temptation to step out of the house a bit and visit nearby. She was eager to wish friends and neighbors a joyous holiday. All went well until she was on her way home. Although the white of the snow provided light, her expectant condition prevented her from seeing a narrow ditch in her path. She slid and fell. Extricating herself from the narrow space was difficult, and she did not wish to risk harming the child within her. It was bitter cold and she was aware of the danger involved. There was no point in screaming. All doors and windows in the neighborhood were shut tightly and the streets were deserted. From afar she could see windows filled with the flickering Chanukah-candle lights. The nostalgic scene added depressingly to her predicament. Time was of the essence. She began to pray.

"Oh, Gracious Master of the universe, this is the month of Kislev, a time designated for miracles! Please grant me a Chanukah miracle, please!"

She pulled herself together and made one more desperate effort again to get out of the ditch. With the help of Hashem she succeeded.

Soon after this incident the baby was born. The birth of a second son filled her with gratitude and joy. She knew the privilege of bringing forth life anew.

In Vilna feverish preparations were made for members of the family to attend the *bris milah*. A huge two-horse-drawn sleigh was hired. As many as could reasonably crowd into it made the trip. The Chazon Ish, his niece, Rebbetzin Alpha, and others were among the excited passengers. Everyone bundled up in the warmest clothing available, and each carried his own blanket to serve as an additional shield against the biting frost. Although the drayman provided blankets, the family preferred to use its own.

The team of horses hitched to the sleigh galloped off at a lusty pace. The speed of the open sleigh skimming the surface of the snow added to the wind's apparent velocity, and the blankets did not keep the cold from penetrating to the bone. After a while some of the more delicate youngsters began to whine plaintively. They were quieted by the elders with promises of warm relief at the first inn ahead. One nephew addressed the Chazon Ish and queried innocently, "What does an inn look like inside, Uncle?" No answer was forthcoming. It was known better than to ask the Chazon Ish the same question twice. He doubtless had heard it the first time and was not to be disturbed further. Out of respect, no one uttered another word.

The horses too felt the cold. But they were in a better position to do something about it. They simply accelerated their pace and thereby increased their warmth. The sleigh seemed to fly. Suddenly, as the horses rounded a sharp curve, the sleigh swerved crazily, lifting one of its runners off the ground. Many of the children were unceremoniously thrown out, falling and tumbling into the mounds of snow like so many drunkards who had lost their equilibrium. The softness of the snow cushioned their fall and prevented injury, but when they tried to rise, they only fell back into the snow-filled trenches along the road.

The drayman was at first unaware of what had happened. Upon learning of the mishap, he brought his team of horses to a halt, reversed direction and returned to retrieve the children. By the time all the travelers were again seated in the sleigh and heading again toward their destination, they were all frozen. Yet for the moment the thrill of having been rescued allowed everyone to forget his discomfort. When the excitement had dwindled, it was fatigue that took hold, and no one had the strength to complain. Strangely enough, it was the Chazon Ish who broke the silence. Turning to his young nephew, he said, "Now you know from personal experience what an inn looks like inside."

It was not in keeping with the Chazon Ish's serious manner to engage in humorous asides. At the same time he was always careful to provide an answer to any question put to him. It mattered little who happened to ask the question or how trivial it seemed. A question deserved a clear and forthright reply. At this time, however, the Chazon Ish hoped to amuse the children by comparing their chilling experience of falling helplessly into mounds of snow to that of out-of-control drunkards in an inn. Unfortunately circumstance afforded an appropriate metaphor.

The excitement of finally reaching their destination compensated for the hardships that had been encountered en route. The *bris milah* was of course the culmination and the highlight of the eventful trip. The baby was named Yehoshua Tanchum.

The elated couple were thrilled with their baby and delighted with the guests who had come to partake in the great joy of the child's entry into the covenant of Abraham. But nothing added more joy to the event than the presence of the Chazon Ish. Rebbetzin Batya considered it a special privilege to have the Torah giant at little Yehoshua Tanchum's *bris*. It was a great honor — a *kavod* — for all. Rebbetzin Rasha Leah shared her daughter's sentiment.

❀ ❀ ❀

More than a Grain of Salt

THE LIFE STYLE THAT REBBETZIN BATYA had hoped to pursue was hampered by her troublesome and weak heart. Some damage must have remained from a childhood disease. From time to time, this restrained and limited her activity. Her selfless care of her husband, which enabled him to learn without disruption and with complete peace of mind, plus her ceaseless toil and devotion in the raising of her two sons were a heavy burden. Her weakened heart could not take the strain, and at one point she simply lacked the strength to continue and fell ill. Immediately Rav Nochum Meir took over. In order to support his wife and children, he moved his family from Kossova to Mishella, a small town in the vicinity of Vilna where he became the spiritual leader of the community.

Although the well-being of his family and the spiritual needs of his congregants were of primary concern to him, he nevertheless invested most of his energy into keeping his wife happy and insuring against any further deterioration of her health. She was naturally concerned and considerably disturbed by her inability to manage her household. Being unable to provide the appropriate support for her husband's learning needs pained her. The thought of this scholarly and saintly man at work in the kitchen was unbearable. She felt that the children were her responsibility and the kitchen her domain. Rav Nochum Meir's place was in the privacy of his study surrounded by shelves of holy *sefarim*. Very much like her mother before her, Rebbetzin Batya turned in her despair to the Almighty. She beseeched His help.

"Almighty G-d! You have created me a woman and blessed me with a *talmid chacham* for a husband together with dear children. Please have mercy on me and permit me to fulfill my duties. Please grant me the strength necessary to realize my obligations. I want only to be faithful to my calling."

Well aware of his wife's anguish, Rav Nochum Meir was anxious to relieve her of the tension. The common faith they shared was instrumental in putting her at ease. It was not difficult to convince her that Hashem was fully cognizant of her good intentions and that they were surely taken into account. Rav Nachum Meir assured her that he did not regard peeling potatoes or other kitchen chores as tasks unbefitting him but rather as necessary conditions incident to the promotion of her recovery. If a visit to an ailing individual was a commendable *mitzvah*, then logically how much more laudable was the actual care of such a person. Certainly the conscientious effort to aid and cure an ill mother of little children was meritorious.

During Rebbetzin Batya's illness her husband created a restful and relaxed atmosphere. This undoubtedly helped speed her recovery. His congregants, however, posed problems of a different nature. Handling them required much diplomacy. The difficulties stemmed from an overdose of respect. When the townspeople realized the nature and extent of their rav's problems, they were reluctant to bring their own problems and questions to him. They were sincerely fearful of embarrassing one whose erudition and dignity were incongruous with the performance of mundane household tasks. Such excessive courtesy could have dangerous consequences, and Rav Nochum Meir saw the potential pitfalls involved. The Torah teaches that ignorance is a dangerous breeder of sin. It also charges leadership with responsibility for transgressions committed by the common folk. When leaders devote themselves to this heavy charge, they can succeed in stemming movements that are destructive of Judaism. *"Our leaders are selflessly laden with their responsibilities; there is no wantonness, no immorality, no outcry in our streets"* (Tehillim 144:14).

Rav Nochum Meir was indeed laden with the responsibility for his flock, and he kept close watch over them. His door was always open, especially to the shy and to the needy. Day and night he was ready to clarify points of law, answer questions and make himself available to help resolve matters in dispute.

In the main, however, his essential method was one of teaching by example. Even his household chores became in time legendary lessons. His diligence in the tender care of his sick wife became widely known in Torah circles. In fact, his devotion was so unique that for years thereafter it was cited time and time again as illustrative of the ideal husband's role in the recovery of an ailing wife.

Because of the quiet and unassuming manner in which Rav Nochum Meir regarded and exercised his heavy responsibilities, it was not realized how much his efforts were actually costing him — that is, except by his wife Batya. She knew that his strict schedule of Torah learning was not in any way diminished by his many additional hours of extra-curricular activity at home. She knew that these hours were extracted from time generally allotted to sleep and rest. Often on awaking in the middle of the night, she found the rav alone in his study bent over a *gemara* learning. While proud and gratified by her husband's dedication, his obvious lack of badly needed rest was a matter of great concern to her.

As Rebbetzin Batya slowly regained her strength, she gradually resumed her household duties. One day while she was in the kitchen salting pieces of chicken and placing them on a wooden rack as part of the koshering process, a middle-aged woman entered. She came to ask Rav Nochum Meir a *she'eilah* (halachic question). On the way to the study she passed the open kitchen door and peeked in. Rebbetzin Batya was startled by the woman's indignant outburst, "*Oh vei! Oh vei is mir!* The young rebbetzin does not know how to kosher a chicken? Can you imagine? Our rav actually eats *treifah* meat! Unbelievable! It's terrible! Never in my life have I seen anyone pouring so much salt on the meat!"

Rebbetzin Batya silently wondered how the rav would handle a woman so blatantly ignorant. Surely he would not scold or ridicule her. By the same token he was not in the habit of lecturing to irate individuals. Would he try to impress the lady with his wife's distinguished lineage? Would he react with outrage to the absurdity of the charge? She prayed that he would not.

While still comtemplating Rav Nochum Meir's possible reaction, she heard him say in a calm and quiet voice, "Please don't be upset. Don't be alarmed. With the help of Hashem I shall review the matter carefully and advise my rebbetzin accordingly."

The rav's gentle, considerate approach quickly calmed the woman while warming Rebbetzin Batya's heart. Still, she could not help but be perplexed. She well knew that Rav Nochum Meir was not one to regard promises lightly. Surely he intended to keep his word to the letter. But how? What was there to be looked into? What sort of advice should she expect?

The woman was hardly out of the door when Rav Nochum Meir rushed into the kitchen. He did not wish to put off his commitment for a moment. He walked directly to the wooden rack where the salted chicken pieces lay. He studied them carefully, spending so much time inspecting that it seemed as if the sight was totally unfamiliar to him. Finally, without lifting his head, he remarked in all seriousness, "Batya, please do not be stingy with the salt. Just pour it on well! Just pour it on!"

With that he left the room, as much in a hurry to leave as he was to enter.

Although Rebbetzin Batya was accustomed to her husband's ways, particularly the meticulous care and deliberation that preceded and accompanied all of his deeds, she was nonetheless deeply moved. Yet she said not a word. No compliments were called for. The rav's conduct spoke for itself. Praise would not have been appropriate. Perhaps for the same reasons there was never any outward show of admiration in the Karelitz home. Even without it, everyone knew that a deep and abiding sense of mutual appreciation was there.

CHAPTER NINE

Looking Back

EVEN PAINFUL MEMORIES FADE INTO DIMNESS. The once-popular and inspiring cry of "A war to end all wars!" was quickly forgotten. In a few short years it vanished, as if it were a **Cure Before the Malady** fossil of some forgotten, distant past. The notion that a war had been fought to end all wars, and that the world had been made safe for democracy, proved indeed to be a grand illusion. Neither the victors nor the vanquished troubled themselves very much to make freedom and democracy feel at home in an inhospitable world.

Bitter at their loss and refusing to admit that it was their own lust for power and expansion that had cost twenty-two million lives, an infinite treasure, the Germans sought scapegoats everywhere. But it was not long before most fingers pointed at the Jews. The Jews who had been so patriotic to the false "Fatherland," had contributed so much to Germany's greatness, had shed blood so disproportionately during the Great War — and who were only one percent of the German population — were blamed for the defeat, and anything else that suited the Germans.

The German people turned to nationalism in its most extreme form, National Socialism, as a way to redeem their lost pride. Their aim was world domination. Their political platform called for the elimination of the Jewish people from German national life. It mattered not whether someone was a whole, half or even a quarter Jew. Many assimilated Jews discovered to their horror that Jewish blood flowed in their veins.

By 1933 the Nazis had come to power. Their purpose was to generate and intensify hatred of the Jew into an instrument of national policy for the purpose of inspiring and unifying the German people. In this they succeeded. Never had a regime been more popular or a nation more united in the effort to exterminate the Jewish people. The Nazi thirst for Jewish blood was so overwhelming in its eagerness and so brutal and systematic in its execution that a tired, yawning Nazi was nowhere to be seen. It was a labor of common love.

In the wake of the Holocaust, two new centers of Torah life began to emerge, the United States and *Eretz Yisrael*. Torah life in the *yishuv* had had an old and solid foundation, but it had been besieged and battered by the twentieth century's winds of change. Would the *yishuv* be equal to its new responsibility?

If there was one individual who answered the need of the hour and helped ready the *yishuv* to receive its observant sons and daughters, the survivors of the Holocaust and the future refugees from the Arab countries, it was the quiet and humble Chazon Ish. He was a man of few words. This may explain why it was never precisely clear as to why he felt impelled in 1932 to seek a permit to settle in *Eretz Yisrael*. What urged him to leave the land of his birth, sever cherished ties, part with his widowed mother and close-knit family at that particular time? If the speculation as to the answer was endless, nobody ever doubted that his decision had been Divinely inspired.

The Chazon Ish and his rebbetzin traveled light. Before World War I their material wealth had amounted to little. After the war it amounted to even less. *Sefarim*, manuscripts and important correspondence comprised the bulk of their baggage.

In the summer of 1933 the S.S. Martha Washington carried the Chazon Ish and his rebbetzin to the Holy Land. No headlines hailed their coming. No guns were on hand to salute them. No school children lined the streets waving tiny blue and white flags, as was the custom when dignitaries arrived. The couple had not anticipated a welcoming ceremony and did not feel the lack thereof. As ever, and perhaps more so on this occasion, the Chazon Ish was preoccupied with thoughts of a different nature. So complete was his involvement with the thrilling experience of reaching the land of his forefathers that not even the question as to where he and his rebbetzin would lodge that first night distracted him in the least.

Well before the Chazon Ish had set foot on the holy ground, his whole being was electrified by the mere thought of the good fortune which awaited him. As his ship drew near to anchor just outside the quaint port of Jaffa, his yearning to perform the commandments, particularly those pertaining to the Land of Israel, grew in intensity. Those commandments applicable specifically to the Land could not by their very nature be fulfilled in the Diaspora and were now at last within actual grasp. More than ever he was the faithful servant of his L-rd, ready and eager to perform, even as his physical well-being was left in the repository of his Master and gave him no concern.

The Master's benevolence was commensurate with the trust invested in Him. As the Chazon Ish waited ashore for the lighter bearing his baggage, Reb David Potash, a well-known philanthropist, arrived to welcome the distinguished couple. Reb David had known the Chazon Ish in Lithuania, and when he had learned of the sage's impending arrival, he rushed to Jaffa port to meet him. There he graciously offered his hospitality and assured the pair of his sincere desire to have them stay at his Tel Aviv home for as long as they wished. While accepting the invitation, the Chazon Ish was not one to take undue advantage of such generosity. They stayed only a day or two at the Potash home. Nonetheless the warm welcome at the outset added to the ecstasy of the Chazon Ish as he beheld for the first time the land of Abraham, Isaac and Jacob.

Within a short time, the Chazon Ish learned, to his dismay, that the very commandments which tied the Children of Israel to their soil, and indeed which rendered them worthy of its possession, had been generally either totally ignored or circumvented by convenient gimmicks and fiction. The sorry state of affairs pained him considerably, but he did not despair. He resolved to live in the heart of this spiritual desert and do what he could to nurture and redeem it.

In the middle of the 1920's a small group of chassidic Jews led by Rabbi Yitzchok Gershtenkorn had founded a settlement about four miles northeast of Tel Aviv. The area in the main was desert and swampland. Wolves habitually prowled at night. The swamps were dried and a small number of simple, bungalow-type houses were erected in the open areas. A few thoroughfares, alleyways and dirt paths were carved out of the hilly terrain to facilitate movement and access. In time the settlement grew into a country village called Bnei Brak. The Talmudic name befitted its religious character.

The Chazon Ish was attracted to this sparsely settled village. He regarded the setting as conducive to the ambitious and strenuous task to which he was committed. It would provide him with a quiet retreat and a centrally located base, where he could carry on his scholarly research and writing in a relatively tranquil environment and disseminate Torah in keeping with his humble and unobtrusive manner. His rebbetzin, too, took a liking to Bnei Brak, and the couple moved into a rented two-room apartment.

Now came a time of building, of preparation, of waiting — for a future that all agreed would sorely try the Jewish people. Yet how different were the methods of the Chazon Ish from those of his Zionist fellow settlers.

The Zionists were dedicated to a spartan life. Their emphasis was on the indoctrination of youth with traits of physical bravery in style with the nations of the world. It was commonplace, for example, for teen-age boys and girls to march through the streets of Tel Aviv singing their own praises: "We have strength! This is our faith!"

While the Zionists sought to inculcate into the youth a sense of fearlessness, the Chazon Ish advocated *yiras shamayim* (fear of

*Rechov Rabbi Akiva, Bnei Brak's main street,
during the settlement's early years*

Heaven). He especially believed that children from an early age should be trained and educated to live in constant fear of G-d. He felt that basic to Jewish survival was the self-evident truth that a Jew had nothing to fear but the lack of fear, for only the fear of Heaven protected the Jew. He wanted every Jewish child to know that "a king was not saved by the multitudes of his army; nor was a hero delivered by great might" (*Tehillim* 33:16), but rather "the eyes of Hashem were upon those who fear Him ..." (*Tehillim* 33:18).

To accomplish the practical task of infusing the spirit of *yiras shamayim* into Jewish youth, the Chazon Ish envisioned an independent network of religious schools spread the length and breadth of the land. They would be free of the possibility of government intervention, supervision or control. Everything was to be done to insure a curriculum untainted by secular or political ideology. *Ahavas Torah* — love of Torah — and *yiras shamayim* — fear of Heaven — these were to be the transcending goals.

The Zionists vehemently rejected the Torah concept. They pinned their faith on physical strength and military power. They readied their young men and women to fight — to fight for an independent Jewish state — independent in all respects.

The Chazon Ish, on the other hand, led his followers in a different direction, that of dependence rather than independence. For a Jew was never to be independent. A Jew by birth was subservient to Hashem, and nowhere on earth could he demonstrate such dependence more effectively than in the land of his forefathers. Rabbi Yehudah Halevy, a twelfth-century poet, expressed it aptly:

> Those who are slaves to the times are the slaves of slaves. Only a servant of Hashem is truly free. Therefore my career is to serve Hashem. So declares my soul.

To help the observant adhere to those Torah laws applicable to the Land, the Chazon Ish proceeded to clarify the commandments pertaining thereto and insisted that such commandments be carried out and implemented. He was particularly concerned with the giving of *maaser* (tithes), *shemittah* (allowing the land to lay fallow and rest every seventh year), *orlah* (proscribing the marketing and consumption of fruit picked from trees younger than four years) and *shmiras Shabbos* (sanctification and rest on the Shabbos day). The latter was a complicated matter because electric power and other utilities were manned by Jews who, in time of emergency, may have been employed on Shabbos. Likewise, the dairy industry involved the milking of cows on Shabbos.

The fourth year after the Chazon Ish arrived in *Eretz Yisrael* was a *shemittah* year. The Chazon Ish asked that the land be accorded total rest. The Zionists scoffed at the idea. "Irresponsible lunacy!" they screamed. The religious Zionists were ready to compromise, seeing in the controversy an opportunity to prove that they were not fanatics. They joined their secular brethren who maintained that a starving people simply could not afford the "luxury" of keeping *shemittah*.

Ironically these people had no difficulty understanding the phenomenon when the land rested involuntarily — for example, when the punishment of drought or pestilence imposed its own peculiar type of rest. They understood, too, the "rest" imposed by riots and war. But the simple desire to demonstrate sacrificial faith and trust in the Almighty was not within their reason's grasp. Even when times subsequently changed for the better economically, there was no understanding of the *shemittah* year or the desire for understanding.

Neither the state of the economy nor ridicule and vilification intimidated or deterred the Chazon Ish. Only the dictates of the Torah mattered. The commandment regarding the observance of *shemittah* year was crystal clear. Scripture could not have been more explicit: "Hashem spoke to Moses on Mount Sinai, saying: Speak to the Children of Israel and say to them: When you come into the land that I give you, the land shall observe a Sabbath rest for Hashem. For six years you may sow your field and for six years you may prune your vineyard; and gather in its crop. But the seventh year shall be a complete rest for the land, a Sabbath for Hashem; do not sow your field and do not prune your vineyard. Do not reap the aftergrowth of your harvest and do not pick grapes you set aside for yourself; it shall be a year of rest for the land. The Sabbath produce of the land shall be yours to eat, for you, for your slave and for your maidservant; and for your laborer and your resident who dwell with you" (*Vayikra* 25:1-6).

The fight for Torah and Torah values did not delight the Chazon Ish. All his life he prayed for a time when friction between brothers would cease and the struggle among Jews to further Torah ideals would no longer be necessary. The secret of success, as the Chazon Ish saw it, was in preventive medicine. He therefore prescribed a vast fabric of *ch'darim*, *yeshivos*, Bais Yaakov schools and *kollelim*, where generations of young Jews would be trained not so much to fight for Torah ways but to live them. It was obvious from the start that a loyal team of able and dedicated men was needed to help implement the ambitious and costly projects conceived by the Chazon Ish. Thanks to Divine help, the desperately needed assistance was not long in coming. By 1935 the oldest of the Karelitz brothers, Rav Meir Karelitz, together with

*One manifestation of the Chazon Ish's dream come true,
hundreds of talmidim studying in the world-renowned Ponevez Yeshiva.*

Rav Shmuel Greineman

three brothers-in-law — Rav Shmuel Greineman, Rav Nochum Meir and Rav Yaakov Yisroel Kanievsky — and their families, had left Lithuania for the Promised Land. The group included Rebbetzin Batya and her mother Rebbetzin Rasha Leah. With the exception of Rav Meir Karelitz, all settled in proximity to the Chazon Ish.

🙣 🙣 🙣

WITH THE ARRIVAL IN *ERETZ YISRAEL* in 1934 and 1935 of several branches of the Karelitz family, implementation of the visionary

Partnerships Formed Long Ago plans of the Chazon Ish to implant and strengthen *Yiddishkeit* in the Holy Land commenced with added zest. Rav

Meir Karelitz, eldest of the brothers, took over execution of the ambitious project, plunging into the task with heart and soul. His brother-in-law, Rav Shmuel Greineman, undertook, with equal determination, the extremely difficult assignment of raising funds to provide the wherewithal to embark upon the enterprise. This was done in the face of a world-wide economic depression.

Towards the end of 1935, Rav Greineman, together with his wife, Rebbetzin Tzivia, left for the United States and took up temporary residence in New York City. In a few months he became fluent in English. But whether his appeal was in Yiddish or English, his personal charm and warmth and genuine humility shone through. His complete dedication to the cause he served won immediate and widespread support.

Among the many who were moved and impressed by Rav Greineman was Mr. Abraham Meyers, a self-made, strong-willed American businessman. Mr. Meyers' constancy of purpose was evident in his ceaseless devotion to many Torah causes. He quickly became a staunch supporter of the Chazon Ish. Although totally blind, he had the inner vision and perception to be among the very first American laymen to recognize the greatness and sublimity of the Chazon Ish. His high regard was more than pocket deep. He gave of himself totally and unstintingly in waging a personal campaign on behalf of the Chazon Ish and his cause of Torah and education in the Land of Israel. Thus when he learned of the poor living conditions of the Chazon Ish, he resolved personally to provide the sage with a suitable and dignified dwelling. The Chazon Ish considered his home to be more than adequate and at first refused to accept a proposal to move to more comfortable and spacious quarters. Subsequently he was reluctantly persuaded to move into a small house in Bnei Brak — but only after insisting that his benefactor accept rent on a regular basis. Mr. Meyers and his sons, who had purchased the site and financed the erection of the structure, agreed to take a nominal rental, which they quietly gave to *tzedakah*. The Chazon Ish shared his home with the Steipler Gaon and his family. Thus two Torah giants dwelt in the building Mr. Abraham Meyers provided. This abode, with its enormous concentration of Torah learning, became the heart of Bnei Brak. The city developed around it.

Years later, when Abraham Meyers was lauded for his early recognition of the stature of the Chazon Ish, he would reply, "Never underestimate the vision of a blind man. For Hashem in

The Chazon Ish's home built for him by Mr. Meyers

His everlasting mercy reinforces and intensifies the remaining senses, so that a blind man is enabled to see what others may have missed." This self-evaluation was indeed a fair and accurate representation of the man. Notwithstanding his blindness, or perhaps because of it, Mr. Meyers was well aware of what went on about him. Moreover he had that uncanny faculty, an extrasensory capacity, which endowed him with the ability to select friends and associates with meticulous care and discrimination. One such friend was Reb Elkana (Carl) Austern, of Far Rockaway, New York. Theirs was a lifelong friendship dating back to the early 1900's, when as youngsters on the Lower East Side of New York they were both active in Adas Bnei Yisroel, known also as the Hebrew League.

This was a small group of Torah-observant youths who were influenced by and rallied around Rav Jacob Joseph, known as the *Rav HaKolel*.* In a time when *Yiddishkeit* on the American scene

* Rav Jacob Joseph pioneered integrity and uncompromising *Yiddishkeit* in New York. His name and memory have been sanctified by the *yeshivah* which bears his name to this day. It was the forerunner and model of hundreds of *yeshivos ketanos* and day schools that revitalized Torah learning in every corner of the United States.

Rabbi Yosef Kahaneman, Ponevezer Rav

was rapidly receding in the stampede of European immigrants to become Americanized as completely and speedily as possible, Abraham Meyers and Elkana Austern were drawn together by the then rare and common interest they shared in living according to the mandates of the Torah and in furtherance of Torah causes.

Among other qualities, the uniqueness of Elkana Austern was evident in the inconspicuous and quiet manner in which he conducted his affairs. He was a *baal chesed* and a *baal tzedakah*, and he went to great lengths to assure secrecy in all his charitable activities. Once he was approached in his Manhattan office by the venerable and illustrious Ponevezer Rav, Rav Yosef Shlomo Kahaneman, for a contribution to the Ponevez Yeshivah, which had been reestablished in Bnei Brak with the blessings of the Chazon Ish. The particular time was a hard one, and Reb Elkana was unable to oblige. He explained to Rav Kahaneman regretfully, "I am simply in no position to give at this time."

Instead of pursuing the matter or pleading his cause further, Rav Kahaneman put Reb Elkana at ease, saying, "Don't worry, Reb Elkana. The *Ribbono Shel Olam* helps. Next time I come, you will be in an excellent position to help."

Before departing, Rav Kahaneman reiterated his blessing with the same gentle, reassuring smile, saying again, "Don't worry. It's all right. The *Ribbono Shel Olam* helps. Do not worry, Reb Elkana!"

Rav Elkana related the incident many times as typical of the deep-seated faith and saintly way of the Ponevezer Rav, wishing to impress upon his own sons and other members of his family recognition of those rare qualities of faith and wisdom that were the hallmark of the *gadol*. In the transmission of such recognition, there was a tendency to overlook the extent to which the incident reflected upon Reb Elkana Austern. He was the kind of man who felt keenly the pain of being unable to give.

While no one knew the precise extent of support Mr. Austern manifested for the undertakings of the Chazon Ish, it is safe to assume that he was most generous. In Hashem's benevolent reward, which both Reb Abraham Meyers and Reb Elkana Austern were ultimately to receive, there was proof positive of their substantial involvement.

On his death in 1954, just four months after the loss of the Chazon Ish, Mr. Abraham Meyers acquired in perpetuity a most valuable and coveted piece of real estate. He lies buried in the Bnei Brak cemetery only a few feet from the Chazon Ish, Rav Shmuel Greineman, Rav Nochum Meir Karelitz, the Steipler Rav and other saintly men. Every inch of the ground is holy. Thousands visit these gravesites every year. In the homage and respect paid and in the prayers offered, Reb Abraham Meyers has a share. He is very much part of the scene. As he was a partner in life, so is he in death.

Hashem remembered Elkana Austern as well. The blessings meted out to him — totally unforseeable at the time of his sacrificial giving — were long in coming and arrived posthumously. Man is unaware of the degree to which his deeds affect the course of events, not only during one's own lifetime but for generations thereafter.

❦ ❦ ❦

In the heart of Bnei Brak, on what is known today as Rechov Chazon Ish, above the site of the small hut where the Chazon Ish and the Steipler Rav lived, stands a living and vibrant monument to his memory. It is a *cheder* known as Tashbar.* The noisy, pulsating activity within the four-story building is the realization of a dream come true. Perhaps nowhere are Jewish values in the very young more reinforced nor Jewish survival more securely assured. Tashbar is an old-fashioned *cheder* where boys from the age of three to thirteen learn little else but Torah and *yiras shamayim.* It is probably the most sought-after *cheder* in the world. The enrollment is such that anxious mothers register their sons for admission on the day of their birth, lest they be denied same by reason of the sheer numbers seeking entry.

Tashbar is open all year round. Excepting Shabbos and *Yom Tov,* classes are held daily. There are no extended week-end breaks or a mid-winter recess. The *chofesh hagadol,* the two-month summer vacation, is not part of the school calendar. In theory and practice there is never a vacation from Torah learning. In some cases, learning for the very young has become so ingrained and so habitual that vacations bore them. The spirit of the school is nurtured by the individual rebbe's selfless and complete devotion to Torah. Though inadequately compensated, working long and difficult hours, occasionally forced to skip a pay check — going out on strike is unthought of. They are dedicated *melamdim* who seek only to mold and educate youngsters in the love and practice of Torah.

It is in this particular *cheder* that Reb Elkana Austern reaps his

---

* An abbreviation of the words *tinokos shel bais rabban*, lit., children study at their teacher's home.

Tashbar

reward. In this four-story building there are a number of classrooms in which the gentle, sing-song voice of Reb Elkana's great-grandsons can be heard. That Austern children, rooted in an American background, pray to Hashem and learn Torah on a site hallowed by the memory of the Chazon Ish cannot be attributed to coincidence.

In a strange way Reb Abraham Meyers has a telling share in these Austern children. For it was he who matched the grandparents of these children, a match that he did not find easy to bring about. Yet the satisfaction he derived from the *shidduch* was apparent in his statement, "No amount of money can buy this *mitzvah*."

That unsung deeds may ultimately play a vital role in the tangled web of life's fabric and in the interlocking of relationships was clearly manifest in February, 1978, when Rebbetzin Batya's granddaughter, Sara, and Reb Elkana Austern's grandson, Oren, stood together under the *chupah*. The many relatives and well-wishers who stood on the grounds outside of Kraushar Hall in Bnei Brak witnessing the marriage ceremony had not the slightest notion of the extent to which this union had been aided and fostered by partnerships formed long ago.

CHAPTER TEN
Strength Within Humility

WHEN THE *CHAZON ISH* had left Vilna for *Eretz Yisrael*, Rav Nochum Meir and Rebbetzin Batya were anxious to follow him. They missed his proximity. It was, however, not easy **"Touch Not** to leave a community in which they had **My Anointed** become an integral part. Rav Nochum Meir was needed locally, and his awareness of this **Ones"** complicated matters. He felt an obligation to remain in the absence of compelling reasons otherwise. Of all things, it was secular education that provided the conditions and the impetus to leave.

After World War I, unenforced laws mandating compulsory schooling for all children were dug up and dusted off. Attendance of children in secular schools teaching reading, writing and arithmetic in the national language was made obligatory. Objections that the reading matter to be read was often immoral, false or political propaganda were brushed off. Moreover, intellectual accomplishment was too often measured by the memory and recitation of inane trivia.

To Rav Nochum Meir and Rebbetzin Batya, however, proficiency in the three R's, regardless of the language, was immaterial. To them, not dates but deeds, not culture but Torah ethics, not abstract logic but Divinely inspired Talmudic reasoning were important. They felt that their sons' place was in the old-fashioned *cheder* and not in a state-run, secular-oriented public school. Accordingly in 1934, when little Nissim became of school age, his parents decided to make the move and follow the Chazon Ish to the Land of Israel.

Packing was a tiring chore. Unlike the Chazon Ish, Rebbetzin Batya did not travel light. She was fortunate to have much worth packing. Due to the fact that she had been married after the carnage of World War I, when there were no Germans or Russians in Kossova to plunder and burn everything in their path, her trousseau and household possessions were intact. Still, notwithstanding an understandable feminine attachment to a variety of articles, she did not succumb to crass sentimentality. She packed with care and discrimination. Rebbetzin Batya was well aware of the hardship and deprivation awaiting her and her family in the Holy Land. She expected with good sense to make good use of everything she included in the baggage. She even calculated that fully stuffed, goose-feather quilts would come in handy in the tropical climate of the Middle East — and surprisingly enough, they did.

Rebbetzin Rasha Leah was thrilled with the impending move to the Promised Land. However, her feelings were mixed, and there was deep anguish in her heart. Thirty years before the jet age, distances were far and the times very uncertain. Then too her age was advanced — she was well into her eighties — and this all added up to make parting with two sons, two daughters and their families, a distressing and traumatic experience. The fact that she was to be in *Eretz Yisrael*, surrounded by Rav Meir, the Chazon Ish, three married daughters and their families, did not mitigate her concern for those left behind in the diaspora. Subsequent tragic events in Europe proved her anxiety to be well founded.

Nevertheless, the years Rebbetzin Rasha Leah was to spend in the Holy Land were her happiest. It was in old age that she came into full bloom. The twilight of her life was a time of magnificent realization of worthy accomplishment. The Chazon Ish contributed much to this feeling of fulfillment. His daily visits to his aging mother lengthened her days. To see them together as she basked in the majesty of his Torah wealth was a sight to behold. Indeed, a lifetime of aspiration came to fruition in the *nachas* she had in the final years of her life.

Her daughter, too, attained the highest degree of maturity during the fifty years she resided in Bnei Brak. She was tested incessantly. Yet with every trial she grew in stature.

The acute poverty Rebbetzin Batya faced soon after moving into her two-room apartment in Bnei Brak made the life she had left behind in Lithuania seem luxurious by comparison. Yet she felt no regret. She enjoyed the privilege of being home. As always, she found nothing to complain about, nothing to covet. Hashem knew her needs and provided accordingly. The tiny two rooms on Rav Blau Street were furnished with less than the bare necessities. The furniture she had acquired was not old enough to qualify as antique but worn enough to appear shabby. Yet with her gifted hands and good taste, she managed to imbue her home with charm. Its air of tranquility and contentment generated warmth. One felt good in the Karelitz home.

Outside, the climate was different. There was a feeling of tension in the street. The British armed forces were everywhere. Numerous Arabs roamed the main thoroughfares, a knife or dagger often lurking in their long-robed garments. Refugees, particularly German Jews, were now arriving in increasing numbers. This in turn inevitably stimulated a growing awareness of the plight of hapless brethren left behind in the old country.

Under the circumstances Rav Nochum Meir, in a long black coat and black hat, should not have attracted much attention. One day, however, three youngsters in their teens did take special note of him. It was the kind of attention he gladly would have done without. Rav Nochum Meir was walking on a narrow-winding dirt path a short distance from his home when the three lads spotted him. They plotted to play a practical joke on the old-fashioned Jew. They conspired to trip him and then flee to an observation point a safe distance away to witness what they thought would be a most amusing spectacle. They expected the bearded Jew to stumble awkwardly to the ground and then, upon rising, grab stones from the gutter and hurl them in a rage, shouting, "You rotten scum! Dogs! You vicious Nazis!" or the like.

Rav Nochum Meir did not notice them until they were on top of him. Without warning, two of the boys pushed him, and the third tripped him. Perfect teamwork. Rav Nochum Meir fell to the ground.

It did not take the boys long to learn that they had tripped the wrong man. This was a Jew who under even more dire circumstances was not wont to raise his voice much above a whisper. He surely was not in the habit of throwing things, especially stones. But how were these Jewish children to know all this when they were so far removed from Torah and so far removed from men of the caliber of Rav Nochum Meir?

When they realized that their little prank had failed, they were stunned. They stared at the saintly man they had wronged. They were taken aback by Rav Nochum Meir's initial silence. His was a face which mirrored the Jewish tragedy of two thousand years. The very *Book of Lamentations* seemed to be reflected in his eyes as they asked the question of old, "*Eichah?* How did it all come about? How can a Jewish boy raise his hands against Torah? How does he dare step on his sacred heritage?"

Rav Nochum Meir rose slowly. Then he motioned to the boys to approach him. They obeyed, and an appearance of innocence replaced their mischievous look. They waited respectfully, moved by the rav's total lack of bitterness or wrath. It was obvious that he harbored not the slightest degree of vengeance. For him, his personal honor was not important. The honor of Torah was what counted. The honor of Torah was at stake. In a strange way the boys seemed anxious to hear what Rav Nochum Meir had to say. In his characteristic gentle manner, Rav Nochum Meir asked, "Did you go to synagogue today? Do you put on *tefillin?*"

The questions were perhaps rhetorical. But they went to the heart of the matter. It was the rav's intention to impress upon the boys a basic fact of Jewish life — that the feet which carry a Jew to the *beis midrash* do not kick or trip, and the hand that puts on *tefillin* does not strike another or inflict pain.

Rav Nochum Meir proceeded to invite the boys to his home, and he offered to learn with them. They did in fact respond by visiting him from time to time. One of them did begin to put on *tefillin*. Although the full and ultimate effect of the incident is not known, one thing is certain: The boys did not soon forget it. A lasting imprint on their behavior remained, undoubtedly to their betterment.

The entire episode would probably never have become known had the boys themselves not related it. Rav Nochum Meir surely would not have given the matter second thought or taken time out to recount the unpleasant experience. Indeed so much happened in the lives of Rav Nochum Meir and his rebbetzin that this encounter in perspective seemed of little consequence and need not have been accorded further mention. Yet the incident was not one to be forgotten. It provided a lesson worthy of remembrance and one which was likely to bear fruit for generations to come.

Under the circumstances it was important to make sure that: "The seed of His servants shall inherit the land, and those who love His name shall find their dwelling place therein" (*Tehillim* 69:37).

To speed the realization of this prophecy, Rav Nochum Meir played a significant role in the founding of *Chinuch Atzmai*, the independent religious school system. Its establishment was eventually to prove indispensable in strengthening the Torah community in the face of ever-increasing anti-religious sentiment.

❧ ❧ ❧

AFTER THEIR ARRIVAL IN THE HOLY LAND, nothing was more important to Rav Nochum Meir and his wife than finding suitable

Nutritious Food schooling for their sons. That was foremost on their minds. Their concern was heightened by the fact that fine *yeshivos* outside of Jerusalem were few in number. In this respect, Lithuania had been more accommodating.

Rebbetzin Batya knew that her sons would be spending most of the waking hours of their growing years in *yeshivah*. Nevertheless, her prime requisite was not for spacious, sun-filled classrooms. She looked only for an inspiring rebbe to kindle and maintain the love of Torah in them.

At the time, Bnei Brak was too young a community to fill such needs at all age levels. Thanks to the efforts of the Chazon Ish and his loyal supporters, Yeshivas Tiferes Zion and Yeshivah Navardok were good beginnings. Rav Nochum Meir was, however, anxious to have his sons attend the Lomza Yeshivah in Petach Tikvah, where they could benefit from the tutelage and leadership of the pious and scholarly Rav Yechiel Mordechai Gordon, a *mechanech* in the genuine *Litvishe* tradition. Petach Tikvah, one of the oldest settlements of religious Jews, is only a few kilometers from Bnei Brak. Yet back then the daily commute from Bnei Brak was problematic and costly — but well worth the inconvenience.

With both her sons in *yeshivah* all day, Rebbetzin Batya now had the time and opportunity to devote herself to important organization work. Surely she had the talent, training, brilliance of mind and kindness of heart to be of valuable service. The times could not have been more opportune. *Chinuch Atzmai*, *Kollel Chazon Ish*, Ponevez Yeshivah and other Torah institutions were all in their embryonic stages of development. The fever to advance the cause of piety had caught the imagination of many. Furthermore, Rav Nochum Meir had become the spiritual leader of the Heligman Shul on Rabbi Akiva Street in Bnei Brak, and the founding of a ladies auxiliary would no doubt have been welcomed. In short, the Torah world needed the rebbetzin's involvement.

She, however, was not quick to exchange her little world for the big one. It was her deep-seated conviction that by selflessly caring for her little world she best benefited the big one. She felt that she was dispensable outside of her home but indispensable within it. Her devotion to her family was of paramount importance, because that was her sacred duty.

The absence of her sons from home did not in any way

diminish their mother's concern for them. On the contrary, her vigilance increased. Of great importance to her, for example, was their mid-day meal. Although the boys, as a rule, did not eat outside their home, it was expected that the *yeshivah*, their second home, would be an exception. The cook was known to be a pious woman, quite knowledgeable in the laws of *kashrus*. Nonetheless, Rebbetzin Batya preferred that her sons only eat food that she herself had prepared.

The lack of time precluded the boys' return home each day for lunch, and surely their mother did not want them to disrupt their Torah-learning routine. To take sandwiches from home was not even considered. A hot, cooked meal was needed to nourish boys learning Torah all day long.

Rebbetzin Batya's solution was simple. She prepared her sons' lunches herself. When they were cooked and ready, she preheated a tiny pot or two and placed the little bits of food into them. These in turn she wrapped into towels. Drinks she poured into thermos bottles. After arranging the food carefully in a basket, so that the delicacies kept their heat and the drinks remained cool, she delivered it all in person, traveling every day by public bus to Petach Tikvah. For three years, day in and day out, she repeated this seemingly insignificant mission. For her the chore was never too tedious. On the contrary, it filled her every day with fresh purpose, joy and love.

The boys were sustained by their lunch in more than a mere physical sense. Their mother's boundless love for them accompanied every bite they took. They also were filled with an indelible impression of the sublime worth of Torah, an impression that could be gained most effectively by sacrificial acts of this nature.

There was yet another dimension that the rebbetzin added. This was an outpouring of prayer that went into the planning, shopping, preparation and delivery of the food to her sons. Mothers have always prayed for the well-being of their children. While the usual request was for children to grow tall and strong and learn to become good providers, Rebbetzin Batya begged Hashem to help her sons grow into giants of Torah.

WOMEN WHO KNEW REBBETZIN BATYA intimately recognized her artistry in prayer. They marveled at the effortless manner in which

Before You Sew a Button, Pray

she prayed. She never had to force concentration. The quality and constancy of her thoughts during prayer were directed only Heavenward. She was enabled to accomplish this by being equipped with the necessary piety to know before Whom she stood.

"Be careful," she would advise others, "to repent before you dare entreat the merciful King of Kings!"

Rebbetzin Batya regarded the ability to commune with the Holy One, Blessed is He, as a priceless privilege, a precious gift given to man. That sinful mortals had easy access to the gates of Heaven was to her a miraculous phenomenon. She had abiding faith that even a quiet whisper coming from the heart would be heard by the Divine Presence. No prearranged audience, go-between or special connection was required. At any time of the day or night, rich and poor, old and young alike had the opportunity to knock on the door of the Almighty and be heard. Of this opportunity the rebbetzin availed herself freely.

While she appreciated random or informal prayer, she liked best to use the formal text of the *siddur*. Nothing to her was more elevating than the opportunity to address the Almighty with the ancient prayers, supplications and praises bequeathed to us by such giants as Moshe *Rabbeinu*, Dovid *HaMelech*, Shlomo *HaMelech*, and the *Anshei Knesses Hagdolah* (Men of the Great Assembly). There seemed always to be transcending strength in the cries and joys of old. Rather than impairing their lasting freshness, repeated usage through the ages had crystallized and enriched the holy words, imparting to prayer a value beyond measure in material terms.

Early each morning after Rav Nochum Meir left home to attend *Shacharis* service, his wife generally took time out herself to pray. There was usually thereafter sufficient time to prepare breakfast and set the table. One morning, however, she was caught unprepared. Rav Nochum Meir returned from *shul* while she was still *davening*. Needless to say, she appeared ill at ease, but neither budged nor spoke. Her husband did his best to calm her. He motioned to her to continue slowly, and proceeded to set the table himself, being careful not to neglect any detail.

In the circumstances, one would think the rebbetzin had reason to revel. Certainly Rav Nochum Meir had been most considerate and understanding. He would not begrudge his wife the opportunity to pray at a time when he had just returned from the House of Prayer himself. Nevertheless, she was far from pleased. Being above self-centered considerations, she found nothing to rejoice about. It was not her practice to measure thoughtfulness or recognition deemed due her. She was well aware of Rav Nochum Meir's gentility and solicitude, for he had proven himself time and again. For example, he had never risen from the dinner table without an expression of gratitude to his wife. This was all the more reason to be sure not to neglect her own obligations. Surely she did not wish even for the sake of prayer to shirk such obligations, for that would have defeated its very purpose. In any event, she resolved to ask the Chazon Ish where her duties lay in this respect, knowing well that he would advise in plain and specific terms just what the Torah demanded of her.

Upon the arrival of the Chazon Ish on one of his daily visits to his aged mother, Rebbetzin Batya asked, "What may I neglect in order to pray?"

As always, the Chazon Ish was brief and explicit. "Before you sew a button, pray," he advised.

In one brief sentence the Chazon Ish had summed up his entire outlook on the matter. He made it clear that while prayer took precedence over trivia, such things as a mother's care of a child or a wife's attention to her husband justified the delay of prayer. Because it is the nature of women to proceed from one chore to another, time passing rapidly and unnoticed, a devout housewife is apt to put off prayer in order to sew a single button. She then discovers that the hem is down, the sleeve needs mending, the collar is worn or perhaps the pocket could use a few stitches. And along the way even if her conscience nags her — "Oh, I have not yet *davened*. Oh, I am late . . ." — it often becomes too late to pray at all. In these circumstances it is prudent to pray first and then do the lesser household chores in accordance with the directive of the Chazon Ish, "Before you sew a button, pray."*

The Chazon Ish admired his sister's seemingly simple questions. To him they demonstrated her constant search for *emes*. Not only the shy and humble manner in which she posed her questions impressed him. Perhaps more important was her realization that a question existed in the first instance. Her steadfast refusal to depend upon her own intellect and very knowledgeable background reflected a profound degree of inner modesty. More than anything else, this endeared her to him.

How much the Chazon Ish valued the modesty of a Jewish woman was perhaps best evident in the response he gave when once asked, "What may a young lady do to match the merits of a young man's Torah learning?"

"Let her work on her *tznius!*" he said. The Chazon Ish considered the modesty of a Jewish woman a virtue so vitally important that the efforts in seeking to achieve this goal were a fitting counterpart to the day and night Torah study and toil of the man. Simply put, the home needs Torah, and Torah needs a home characterized by virtue. Rebbetzin Batya was a noble example of the kind of *tznius* the Chazon Ish envisioned. Indeed, he was so touched by her ways in this respect that he was once moved to comment, "Batya, some day women will look to receive your blessings." Years later her brother-in-law, the saintly Steipler Gaon, went a step further when he remarked to her, "You qualify to confer blessings on others."

Rebbetzin Batya Karelitz continued to rise in piety and stature to an astonishing degree. As a result, women from all walks of life came to her with a variety and multitude of problems and questions in the hope of obtaining valuable advice and blessing.

---

* The reader is reminded not to regard anything in this book as a *p'sak halachah*. Incidents are related solely for the purpose of illustrating the need to pose questions and rely only upon proper halachic authority. Every situation is unique and is to be judged on its own merits.

The Steipler Gaon

Her door was always open, and her ear and heart absorbed in tale after tale of torment and suffering. She listened to every story with understanding, compassion and concern. With all her heart she wished to help.

The task of conferring blessings upon others, however, went somehow against her grain. Although she never deemed herself worthy of such a mission, she nevertheless made a genuine effort to help with every situation by humbly beseeching Hashem to have mercy and speedily grant the wishes of those who sought her aid.

In 1978 a five-year-old boy requiring complicated brain surgery was taken from Israel to Zurich, Switzerland, where Dr. Jafargil, a renowned surgeon, performed the operation. For some time following the child's return home, he needed constant and careful supervision. He was not permitted to run about for fear that undue exertion would harm him. A periodic visit to Rebbetzin Batya was one of the child's most pleasurable treats. The little boy loved her dearly. With unbelievable patience and affection the rebbetzin entertained her little visitor and made him feel as if his visit was terribly important to her. On one such occasion the child approached her and begged, "Please give me a blessing." Deeply moved, Rebbetzin Batya asked that Hashem grant him a complete recovery so that he may return to *cheder* as soon as possible and learn lots and lots of Torah. As the little boy was about to leave, she beckoned to him to linger a bit longer, and quietly said, "And now, you give me a blessing!"

CHAPTER ELEVEN
Remember — Do Not Forget

IF WORLD WAR II WAS A TRAGEDY FOR MANKIND, it was a much greater one for the Jewish people. The Germans aspired not only to annihilate them but to torture them to death.

The Offerings Were of the Finest Their savagery was such that it was difficult to understand how Rebbetzin Batya, for example, could live with the knowledge that brothers and sisters and their families, relatives and friends were being hideously murdered. In a strange way she and countless other Jews were undoubtedly numbed by the sheer immensity of the national tragedy, which dwarfed and subordinated the loss and suffering of the individual.

"If My sons forsake My Torah and do not walk in the ways of My ordinances; if they profane My statutes and do not keep My commandments, then I shall punish their defection with the rod and their iniquity with wounds" (*Tehillim* 89:31-33).

Unfortunately this warning was familiar only to those who were steeped in Jewish tradition and whose perspective had been forged in the crucible of history. They knew that a Jew did not suffer because he was Jewish, but rather because he was not Jewish enough. They knew too that Jewish redemption and Jewish survival depended upon increased piety and more widespread obedience to *mitzvos*.

All her life Rebbetzin Batya scrutinized in advance every move she made, knowing that deeds were a matter of life and death. At a time when her people were downtrodden and ruthlessly persecuted, and the lives of brothers and sisters and their families were being threatened, there was a need to intensify every effort and mobilize all strength available in Hashem's service. Thus she clung to the ways of her G-d as never before. With all the zeal she could muster, she poured her heart and soul into supplication and prayer. As never before, she petitioned her Father in Heaven to be merciful and gracious in granting salvation to His children. She continuously entreated Hashem. She would not let go. How could she when the House of Israel was aflame and the need to move heaven and earth was so desperate? Yet through all the trials and tribulations of the times, her spirit remained humble. In fact, the greater the pain, the more humble was her plea. There was no shortage of prayer to express her feelings:

"With all Thy lovingkindness, stun my enemies and destroy the oppressors of my soul, because I am Thy servant" (Tehillim 143:12).

"How long shall the lawless, Oh G-d, how long shall the lawless rejoice?" (Tehillim 94:3).

"Master of the universe, it is not merit that is the basis of our plea before Thee but rather Thy compassion. For what are we? What is our life? ... What is our righteousness? ... What is our strength?" (Morning prayer).

"Oh, behold! As the stone is in the hand of the mason, who at his will retains it or breaks it into pieces, thus are we in Thy hand" (Yom Kippur prayer).

There was a profusion of prayer and there were streams of tears and rivers of blood before the madness came to an end. The German army in North Africa was stopped in its tracks in 1943 while racing toward the Holy Land. The tide of war had turned. Field Marshall Montgomery, commander of allied forces at El Alamein, was not aware of the role that Rebbetzin Batya's prayers and those of many other pious Jews had played in the victory.

When peace at last returned, it was time to take inventory.

Families sought out loved ones in the DP camps and in the lists published in the papers. The numbing effect of years of war was replaced by the grim reality of the terrible losses that had occurred and the staggering price in human life that had been paid. Nothing told the story more vividly than the dreaded questions that had to be asked. Those who had managed to survive sought the answers: Who was yet alive? Who had been put to death? Who by the sword and who by fire? Who by wild beasts and who by starvation? Who by strangulation and who by drowning? Who had been injected with disease germs and who had frozen to death? Who had been gassed and who had been buried alive? The queries were endless.

Like others in *Eretz Yisrael* who had come from Europe, the Karelitz family made the necessary inquiries as to missing kin and waited with trepidation and fear for some news. Rebbetzin Rasha Leah had been spared even the knowledge of the ordeal of the war. Her soul had departed in October, 1940, before German armed forces had marched into Lithuania. She had been spared the agony of knowing that two sons, two daughters and their entire families with the exception of one grandson had been massacred in cold blood. She never lived to learn that Kossova was to be totally bereft of its Jewish population — Kossova, where she had grown up; where her father, husband, son-in-law and son had served as spiritual leaders of the community; where all of her children had been born and raised; and where the only remnants of a glorious past were soon to be rows of Jewish tombstones and mass graves. Yet Kossova was never completely obliterated. It will long be remembered as the birthplace of her illustrious son, the Chazon Ish. Rebbetzin Rasha Leah's contribution to that end long before her son was born may not be remembered, but it was nonetheless very real.

❧ ❧ ❧

While yet a child of ten, Rebbetzin Rasha Leah admired the many well-known sages and *maggidim* who were wont to travel from town to town inspiring Jews with Torah wisdom. Invariably they drew enthusiastic crowds into the synagogues and kept their listeners galvanized not only to their seats but to their faith as well. These saintly men of learning were often Shabbos or overnight guests at the Kossova rav's home. Rasha Leah, the rav's oldest child, catered to them and made them feel at home. So sincere and dedicated was her servitude that one of the *maggidim* was impelled to ask, "How may I repay your kindness, *meidele*? What can I do for you?"

Without hesitation Rasha Leah responded shyly, "Please give me a blessing."

"What kind of blessing would you like me to give you?" the old man asked with good-natured interest.

"I would like to be blessed with many sons, all of them very great *talmidei chachamim*," she replied instantly.

The *maggid* was taken aback by the unbelievable maturity of this young girl. Surely he had expected a request of a different nature. Without delay and with a full heart the saintly man bestowed upon Rasha Leah his blessing, which she truly desired and deserved.

During the ninety years of her life she was constantly in the company of the finest of Torah scholars. Near the end, when she was too weak to bear the humid summer climate of Bnei Brak, she was taken to the holy city of Jerusalem. Here she spent her last months with her eldest son, Rav Meir Karelitz. It was fitting that Rav Meir, who had become the first to personify her lifelong dream of Torah-steeped sons, should be at her side when the end came.

The bereaved children mourned her passing deeply. They keenly felt the void. Their grief was punctuated by more than cherished remembrances of bygone days. Rebbetzin Rasha Leah had infused and solidified the family into a unit too strong to be severed by death. The Karelitz family had been aware of this oneness even when they were still little children. It was recalled that once when two of the Karelitz boys were on their way home from the *beis medrash*, they were frightened by someone and began to run. Before reaching home, they both tripped and fell.

One scraped his knee; the other bruised his chin. As their mother tended to their wounds, one of them asked, "What hurts you more, Mommy, your chin or your knee?" The children had simply forgotten their pain and were concerned about their mother. They were always much a part of her and she a part of them.

This strong tie of kinship and unity within the Karelitz family became a disadvantage, however, when Rebbetzin Batya learned of the horrors that had befallen her family. Details of the atrocities that had been perpetrated reached her gradually and in fragments. When the pieces were all together, the picture was a grim one.

Rav Shmuel Eliyahu Kahan, her brother-in-law, had been one of the very few spiritual leaders who had succeeded in uniting the *chassidim* and *misnagdim* into a single congregation. Together with her sister, Badana, he stood at the fore as they were marched out of the town of Ortasha to their deaths. They were much loved and esteemed by their congregants whose fate they shared. Surely the presence of Rav Kahan and his rebbetzin at this critical hour helped lessen their fright and fired them with the faith of the forefathers. Rarely before was it so vital to have on hand a man of peace and spirit in the face of evil and violence. Heaven was surely moved by the contrast.

Rav Moshe Karelitz, her youngest brother, together with his wife and family and congregants, were all massacred, much in the same fashion as Rav Kahan and Rebbetzin Badana had been. Those who related the events said that Communist partisans had offered Rav Moshe the opportunity to escape, but he had refused. Like Rav Kahan, he preferred to share the common fate of his co-religionists and together with them and his entire family went to his premature death.

There had been an especially close relationship between Rebbetzin Batya and her brother-in-law, Rav Abba Swiatycki, because he and her oldest sister, Enya Chaya, had remained in Kossova after they were married. During the years of the First World War, Rebbetzin Batya had had the opportunity to know him well. She often remarked how, during those difficult war

Rav Shmuel Eliyahu Kahan

years, he had given his allotted portion of food to a starving child. In 1927 Rav Abba Swiatycki relinquished his post as spiritual leader of Kossova in favor of his brother-in-law, Rav Yitzchok Zundel, and transferred to the city of Tiktin. In 1942 the Germans assembled all the Jews of Tiktin in the town square to be killed. Rav Abba Swiatycki and Rebbetzin Enya Chaya stood in the forefront of the congregants. Every Jewish soul, to the last man, woman and child, was murdered in cold blood. The only member of the family who managed to survive was Rav Swiatycki's only son, Chaim. In miraculous circumstances he succeeded in reaching the Land of Israel in 1938. Perhaps in the merit of his father's compassion for starving children in World War I, there was intervention from Above in World War II.

Her third brother, Rav Yitzchok Zundel Karelitz, was singled out by the Germans for special treatment. Soon after they occupied

Rav Abba Swiatycki

Kossova, German soldiers went on a wild shooting spree, and shot Rav Yitzchok Zundel to death in his own home. His wife and daughter witnessed the murder. Distraught and pained, they jumped unnoticed onto the van carrying away the remains of the deceased and others who had been butchered to death. The van was driven to a mass gravesite. Mother and daughter were never seen or heard from again.

The deep affection that Rebbetzin Batya had for each and every member of her family made news of the losses almost unbearable. It tore and wrung the heart. Yet she suffered in silence. Never did a word of complaint escape her lips. Her unshakeable faith in the everlasting benevolence of the Almighty kept her weak heart beating. To her it was crystal clear that *Am Yisrael* had been required to sacrifice, and the offerings taken had to be of the finest and the purest.

Open House

RAV NOCHUM MEIR'S FIRST COUSIN, Rav Yehoshua Berkman, had lived in Telz, Lithuania before World War II. He and his wife and children, together with virtually the entire population of the town, had been mur-

Born to Belong dered by the Germans. Only a few days before the massacre, two of his daughters, Batsheva, fourteen, and Shoshana, thirteen, had managed to escape. They were taken in by gentiles, who, at great personal risk, hid and sheltered them for the duration of the war. Especially kind to these orphaned girls was the royal Narutovitz family.

At war's end the sisters emerged from hiding only to learn that they had no home to which to return. Loss of family, relatives and friends had drained any feelings of attachment to their native land. But where were they to go and what were they to do? Their choice was the only sound alternative available — to endeavor to reach the home of their forefathers.

On learning of their decision, Rebbetzin Batya readied her tiny apartment in Bnei Brak to receive them. To provide a warm home for the two girls, bereft of family and friends, was her fervent wish. She perceived in their coming the possibility of gaining in one stroke two daughters, something that had been denied her. But the route which the girls were yet to travel before reaching the Promised Land was a long and difficult one.

Although the Germans had capitulated on the 8th day of May, 1945 and the war in Europe was officially over, the Holocaust had not terminated. For many of the survivors, more dead than alive, liberation came too late. For example, long after the war had ended, an untold number of Jews continued to die in Bergen-Belsen, due to dysentery, malnutrition and lack of medical care.

The liberating armies, reflecting government policy, were generally indifferent to the plight of the distressed, and kept them in Displaced Persons Camps — subject to regimentation and limited freedom of movement. Professionals were unable to practice their professions; skilled workers their trades; and the unskilled were denied a chance to learn a useful occupation. Thousands languished in idleness and boredom without guidance or direction and short on hope or ambition. It was not that these refugees sought or expected a hero's welcome or a ticker-tape parade. Far from it. They wished only the opportunity to begin life anew in a suitable and civilized environment.

The world was generally insensitive to the woes of these people. Switzerland, for example, sealed her borders to Jews and other refugees, while Russia prevented her Jews from leaving. At the same time the British decided that the same Jews had no legitimate claim to their ancestral homeland. They embarked upon a policy of excluding Jewish immigration to Palestine while simultaneously overtly patronizing the Arabs. The Americans were generous, but not with a full heart. Enforcing a system of strictly limited immigration quotas, they were slow to process immigration applications and often demanded documents which most refugees could not produce. Immigration to the United States was a frustrating experience. The Americans were openhanded in their humanitarian efforts, but they failed to realize that hand-outs alone were not a cure-all or panacea. When Jewish survivors took steps to address the deplorable situation, they were met with obstacles every inch of the way.

The road that Batsheva and Shoshana braved from Lithuania to *Eretz Yisrael* was accordingly anything but a pleasure tour. It was remarkable that two young girls, who had in the recent past withstood so much suffering and misfortune, possessed the physical and spiritual stamina to infiltrate illegally in and out of hostile countries until at long last they were able to reach their destination.

Shoshana, the younger of the two, was the first to make it to the Holy Land. While waiting in Italy for illegal transport by sea to *Eretz Yisrael*, she was fortunate enough to obtain a children's certificate that enabled her to enter legally. As the result of a magnanimous gesture by the British, five hundred entry permits had been issued for the benefit of Jewish youth under the age of fourteen. The Germans, however, had been less than accommodating, inasmuch as it was found impossible to assemble five hundred living Jewish children less than fourteen years old. In the circumstances boys and girls in their upper teens became eligible recipients of the coveted papers. Shoshana was one of them.

Four difficult months later in 1946, Batsheva reached the shores of her new homeland. Her entry, however, was not as respectable as her sister's. Under cover of darkness she and a shipload of Jewish refugees, eluding British gun-boats and beach patrols, managed to wade ashore like so many thieves.

After Batsheva's arrival, Rav Nochum Meir met the girls and advised them of his wife's intention to provide them with a home. Following a protracted period of processing, registration and considerable red tape, Batsheva and Shoshana arrived in Bnei Brak.

Rebbetzin Batya tried to persuade them to stay with her. The girls were obviously uneasy. They found themselves in an unpleasant situation. While they were moved by her earnest and deep-seated desire to make her home theirs, they could readily see that there was absolutely no room for them. Indeed they were puzzled by the rebbetzin's insistence when the apartment simply lacked the facilities and space to house them. Rebbetzin Batya's eyes read the girls' thoughts.

"There is room," she said emphatically in an added effort to reassure them. "There is room. Of course there is room!" she continued with feeling. "And if there isn't room, we will make room. We will find a cozy spot for you in the hallway or so.

It is not important where you sleep, but rather how well you sleep."

She turned to Batsheva, who had managed to get a job as a supervisor of girls in an absorption center, and said, "Work anywhere you wish, work all day long, but when the work is done, come home! A girl needs a home! A girl needs to know that she belongs! A fine Jewish girl's place is in the home, because she was born to belong!"

These words made a strong and lasting impression. Batsheva and Shoshana yielded to Rebbetzin Batya's blandishments and moved in with their meager belongings. They remained under Rebbetzin Batya's loving care and tutelage for a long time.

By any standard their sleeping quarters were not luxurious. But their sleep was sweet nonetheless, and they enjoyed a peace of mind and a tranquility they had not experienced since their escape from Telz. This was due to the thoughtful and dedicated manner with which Rebbetzin Batya cared for them. Her presence and spirit permeated the home and made it what it was.

While everyday life may have seemed routine, there were many unexpected and unsolicited kindnesses that were telling in their impact. Whether it was a simple word of greeting or a more serious word of *mussar*, Rebbetzin Batya had a way that moved the heart. What she said came from the heart and was rendered with tact and understanding. She took an active interest in the girls, the same interest that any *Yiddishe mamme* would take in her own daughters. She did it without appearing to be inquisitive or unduly officious. The relationship developed into an intimate one, and the girls would readily confide in her whenever the need arose.

One day Batsheva came home irate and bitter and took her troubles to Rebbetzin Batya. "Some girls at the center are catty!" she announced, fuming. She would have proceeded to pour out her heart in search of sympathy, but the rebbetzin interrupted her.

"Oh, Batsheva," she said in her characteristically soothing manner. "Why care? Please forget this nonsense. Why measure every word, every move? Don't we have enough problems?"

This gentle approach was effective, and Batsheva's fury,

however intense only moments earlier, subsided instantly. The sheer sweetness of Rebbetzin Batya's voice had a calming influence and made Batsheva realize that she had been petty. She regretted having made the fuss.

Once, in the midst of koshering her chicken, Rebbitzin Batya accidentally pricked her finger, and contact with salt burned her painfully. She asked Shoshana to continue the salting while she watched and supervised. A few hours later, she poured a bit of fresh chicken soup with chunks of meat in it into a small pot and said to Shoshana, "The Chazon Ish is very weak. Perhaps a little bit of soup and meat will do him good. Let us go and take it to him." As always Shoshana was elated with the opportunity, but this time, she felt a special pride. "I helped kosher this meat for the Chazon Ish!" It had become a privilege never to be forgotten.

Rebbetzin Batya was extremely careful to avoid even the appearance of favoring her two sons. When the girls returned home, they found the table nicely set for four. Each plate contained some of the tasty delicacies that she had thoughtfully prepared. The distribution of food, like the distribution of tender loving care, was always evenhanded. She went to great lengths in repeatedly demonstrating that the orphans were as dear to her as her own sons. It did not take long for Batsheva and Shoshana to know without a question that they belonged.

The harmonious life within the Karelitz home seemed to be constantly threatened by the goings-on without. There was no end to the shedding of Jewish blood. The Germans had murdered outright the infants and young children, the feeble, the crippled and the elderly. Only the physically fit had some chance of survival. World War II had hardly ended when this surviving remnant was called upon in *Eretz Yisrael* to bear arms to protect the *yishuv* in the face of the Arab menace from within and without. Many young men and boys, fortunate to have survived the atrocities of the Holocaust, reached the shores of their homeland only to die on its battlefields. Even after the war with the Arabs had been successfully concluded at a frightful cost in Jewish blood, the uncertainty of how much more would have to be spilled remained. In spite of the miraculous victory and the never-ending uncertainties, most Jews were still blind to the fact that they do have a mighty Protector to turn to:

> "Oh, that My people would hearken to Me; that Israel would earnestly walk in My way! How speedily would I subdue their enemies and turn My hand against their oppressors" (*Tehillim* 81:14-15).

When the War of Independence was over and life had normalized somewhat, Rebbetzin Batya was most anxious to find suitable husbands for Batsheva and Shoshana. She thought it most important that the girls build their own homes and families. In those times marrying was a simpler affair than it is today. One did not have to be wealthy to provide a young couple with basic essentials and a start in life. It was not necessary to pay a fortune to purchase a tiny apartment. Life was a struggle, but marriage with dignity seemed to come more easily. A fine girl like Batsheva had but to find her match, and that was all.

At that time, the Ponevez Yeshivah in Bnei Brak was just beginning to show its promise. Under the inspiring leadership of the great Ponevezer Rav, Yosef Shlomo Kahaneman, and Rav Eliyahu Eliezer Dessler, *the mashgiach*, it had attracted a number of outstanding *bachurim*. Among the *talmidim* — each a jewel in his own right — were Rebbetzin Batya's two sons, Rav Nissim and Rav Yehoshua Tanchum, and Rav Avraham Schwartz. The latter was found eminently suitable for Batsheva. They met and shortly thereafter were engaged to be married.

Rebbetzin Batya wasted no time. She immediately undertook the arduous and detailed task of preparing for the forthcoming wedding, and she seemed to enjoy every minute of it. One warm and humid day Batsheva was surprised to see the rebbetzin enter her tiny bedroom and shut the window tightly. Then before locking herself into the room she announced cheerfully, "The time has come to make good use of my goose-feather quilts." She smiled and added apologetically, "I must lock the door. Otherwise the slightest draft may play havoc with the feathers." Every feather

seemed precious to her as she seated herself in the airtight room
and opened the quilts. She proceeded to divide the mass of feathers
into eight equal parts, making eight lightweight quilts out of the
two huge ones. The arithmetic was simple and correct: two quilts
for each of her four children.

"Why is Rebbetzin Batya in such a hurry to open both of the
quilts?" Batsheva queried.

"Well," she explained, "when one starts something, it is best to
finish it without delay."

It later became apparent that there was a hidden meaning to this
explanation. In her heart Rebbetzin Batya was hoping for many
more weddings to come. In fact she already had in mind someone
special for her older son, Rav Nissim. As she labored in a sea of
goose feathers, she no doubt looked forward to a very special
meeting.

❀ ❀ ❀

Some nine years had passed since Rebbetzin Batya's sisters,
Rebbetzin Tzivia Greineman and Rebbetzin Miriam Kanievsky,
spent a memorable day in the holy city of Jerusalem. They were on
a special mission that had led them to the home of Rebbetzin
Chaya Kopfshitz. The two women walked the old, narrow,
winding streets in the Mea Shearim quarter, and when they at last
spotted Batei Nathan 7, they knew that they had reached their
destination.

Rebbetzin Kopfshitz welcomed her guests with characteristic
warmth. Although she had not previously met them, they had
heard much about each other. Not only had Rebbetzin Chaya been
married to Rav Tzvi Kopfshitz, a gifted Talmudic scholar, but she
herself was a product of distinguished lineage. She was the favorite
granddaughter of the late Rav Yosef Chaim Sonnenfeld. It was not
likely that the Chief Rabbi of Jerusalem's *Eidah Chareidis*
community and one of world-Jewry's most renowned sages would
favor one grandchild over others unless he recognized unusual
merit in her. Indeed, Rebbetzin Chaya had earned her grandfather's special affection the hard way.

Rav Yosef Chaim Sonnenfeld had suffered great personal misfortune during his lifetime. One of his married daughters had passed away at a very young age, leaving a large family of orphaned children. Eleven-year-old Chaya was one of them. The sudden loss of her mother had matured Chaya far beyond her years, inasmuch as it was she who assumed the management of the entire household. With unbelievable devotion she looked after all of her older and younger sisters and brothers. A few years later tragedy struck again with the death of her married sister. Chaya took in her sister's orphaned little daughter Leah and raised her.

By nature Chaya was always cheerful. All the hardship and poverty that she had endured never had a depressing effect upon her. Only once did she find cause to complain. When her time had come to marry, her trousseau included no pillows. This bothered her a great deal, and in desperation she took her problem to her illustrious grandfather.

"Grandfather," she said, distressed, "my wedding day is approaching, and I don't have the means to buy pillows. How does a bride get married without pillows?"

Rav Sonnenfeld pondered the question a moment or two. He then asked, "Where is it written in the Torah that a bride must have pillows in order to get married? G-d willing, you will raise a fine family with or without pillows."

Chaya was grateful for the blessing she had received, and was never again troubled by the want of pillows. True to her grandfather's blessing, she managed well to raise several of her own children and her niece Leah in a one-room apartment in Mea Shearim.

At the time of this visit Leah had grown into a beautiful young girl of eighteen. It was this Leah who was the object of the visit that day to the Mea Shearim home of Rebbetzin Kopfshitz.

Rebbetzin Greineman and Rebbetzin Kanievsky were deeply moved by the atmosphere of genuine *chesed* in the Kopfshitz home and made no secret of the fine impression they had gained. As they were about to leave, Rebbetzin Miriam somewhat startled her hostess by taking particular note of a little girl standing shyly at the opposite end of the room. "How old is your little girl?" she asked.

"Oh," replied Rebbetzin Chaya, "she is my daughter Leah. We have a big Leah and a little Leah. The little one is almost eight." She did not attach much significance to the query.

"If Hashem will be willing," Rebbetzin Miriam added in all seriousness, "we shall return in ten years and ask you to give us this little girl of yours as well."

The remark brought a smile to Rebbetzin Chaya's face. She appreciated the gesture but eventually forgot about it.

❦   ❦   ❦

Ten years later it was Rebbetzin Batya who came to visit and to ask for little Leah. She got what she came for. While ten years is a long time in the formative stages of a young girl's life, Rebbetzin Batya was not overly concerned about changes that could have occurred. She was confident that the traits that her sisters had perceived in that eight-year-old girl were, considering the circumstances of home and environment, not given to change. Throughout the ensuing years she had often thought of that little girl from Mea Shearim growing up in a home where unusual *chesed* and love of Torah were the touchstones of life. She desired nothing less for her son Nissim.

Meanwhile Batsheva came first, and Rebbetzin Batya was busy sewing, cooking and baking. The work was almost endless. And even though her own possessions were meager and few, she somehow managed to find "treasures" stashed away which she could do without and which Batsheva could make good use of.

On the day of the wedding, everything was ready as planned. The tables were all set in good taste and the general mood was one of festivity. Rebbetzin Esther (Greineman) Finkel arrived early. She had come straight from work just in case her help was needed. Upon entering her parents' home, where the wedding was about to take place, she was touched by the display of goodness that shone through all the niceties. She found Rebbetzin Batya busily engaged in an attempt to transform an old piece of borrowed furniture into an elaborate bridal chair. She had managed to procure some remnants of silk, satin and shantung, and with her artistic talent was fashioning a pattern as she covered the shabby wood and the worn upholstery. Esther watched her admiringly. It was obvious that much thought and love had accompanied the effort. Her aunt suddenly looked up. Noticing Esther's presence and eyeing her attire, she made no secret of her displeasure.

"Is this how you come dressed to a wedding?" she asked in a scolding tone of voice. "Please change and put on your very best dress."

Esther did not say a word. She knew that if there was a note of acerbity in the request it was meant well.

Rebbetzin Batya shook her head and continued disapprovingly. "This is how you come dressed to Batsheva's wedding? I am surprised at you, Esther. Do you not know who is getting married today? An orphan is getting married. We must make her feel important. Don't you see? A *yesomah* is getting married!"

❧   ❧   ❧

The Secret

REBBETZIN BATYA, IN A VERY LITERAL SENSE, kept an open house. She had no locks or burglar alarms attached to her door. Visitors came and went at all hours of the day and late into the night. Her open invitation contained no time restrictions. No one ever arrived too early or too late — just on time. The rebbetzin managed this hospitality because she was never in a hurry. She always seemed to have plenty of time. She never felt that she was losing out by giving of her time to others.

Among the women who frequently visited Rebbetzin Batya was a young lady who seemed to be burdened by a lasting predicament. She had been married for many years without being blessed with a child. This problem gave her no peace. The rebbetzin's soothing manner and deep faith filled the young woman with hope and gave her relief. She came often.

After being barren for sixteen years the young woman suddenly discovered that she was expecting. Elated, she rushed to tell the news to Rebbetzin Batya.

"It is a secret, a big secret," she began shyly. "But I want Rebbetzin Batya to be among the very first to know. Hashem has blessed me. Yes, Hashem has had mercy on me. I am with child," she said happily.

"*Baruch Hashem, Baruch Hashem*," Rebbetzin Batya whispered gratefully. Her heart was full of gratitude.

"I think it is best to keep the good news secret for as long as possible," the young woman said cautiously.

Rebbetzin Batya nodded her head in agreement. As always, she encouraged silence. She saw the possibility of harm in unnecessary talk and publicity and was quick to advise against the perils of the tongue. As always, she was an ideal model for her teachings. For no matter how deeply moved she was by Hashem's benevolence, she hid her feelings.

Some months later the young woman returned. This time she wore a becoming maternity dress. Her facial features were relaxed, her eyes beamed and her disposition was cheerful. Rebbetzin Batya was gladdened by the dramatic change that had taken place both inwardly and outwardly. The young woman sat down and described the wonderful experience of feeling life within life. The rebbetzin offered her some sound and practical advice concerning the different stages of pregnancy. Both guest and hostess seemed to be enjoying the conversation.

When the young woman rose to leave, Rebbetzin Batya ventured a request she had on her mind for some time: "Now that most everyone knows the good news, may I reveal it to my husband, the rav? Rav Nochum Meir will be happy to hear the good tidings. May I tell him?" she begged, as if wishing to be released of an oath.

The young woman stood speechless, wondering: How sacred could a simple secret be?

❀ ❀ ❀

A PROMINENT LADY PSYCHIATRIST was once caught in the midst of a lively conversation with herself. Startled and embar-

The Spoken Word rassed, she rushed to explain: "I am in the habit of talking to myself because no one else listens to what I have to say. There certainly is no shortage of talkers but who listens? Who heeds the spoken word?"

She stopped to catch her breath, then added, smiling sarcastically, "I deal with a number of people who fall asleep while a barrage of blabber pounds their eardrums. Talk too often lulls the senses more effectively than sleeping pills. If you ask me, most of the energy invested in advertising or the like is wasted. So few listen! So few listen!"

The woman managed to spotlight a tragic truth. Speech has too often lost the dignity, purpose and value for which it was created. Indeed, there are few who know when to speak, what to say, how to listen, and when to be silent. Rebbetzin Batya was one of those few. She achieved this mastery by constantly talking to herself. Silently, without uttering a word, she would speak to her heart and the heart listened. All her mature life she studied and restudied books of *mussar* in order to refine her inner speech.

In the month of Elul, when Jews are traditionally aroused to look inward, the flow of women waiting to see Rebbetzin Batya increased considerably. Rebbetzin Aliza Zeichner of Bnei Brak was one of them. How much she was moved by the reverential awe she felt in the presence of Rebbetzin Batya was evident from the lessons she sought at a time when guidance was crucial.

"If you could only teach me to pray with the necessary deliberation," she begged.

Like most pious women, Rebbetzin Aliza was inspired by the beautiful Rosh Hashanah and Yom Kippur prayers. Her soul yearned to offer supplication with the utmost deliberation. But how difficult it is to hold fast to prayer when distractions abound! How tempting to snatch an occasional glimpse aside! How easy it is for the mind to drift away, reducing prayer to lip service. She wanted to know: How does one develop and retain the power of concentration in these circumstances?

The answer, as always, was short and to the point: "Make an effort to hear the words you speak," Rebbetzin Batya advised. To her, the solution was simple. She had trained her heart to obey the dictates of her mind, and the mind respected the wishes of the heart. There was no conflict within. Her concentration in prayer was blessed with inner harmony, so that her thoughts and her heart joined in common effort. No matter how crowded the synagogue or how elegant her neighbor, she was not aware of it. When she prayed she was alone with her Master. Nothing else mattered.

Once at the conclusion of *Shemoneh Esrei*, Rebbetzin Batya was tired and had to sit. Her eyes were still fixed upon the *siddur* and her thoughts deep in concentrated devotion when she slowly lowered her body, not realizing that there was no chair behind her. Fortunately several women nearby were quick enough to catch her and prevent a fall and serious injury.

In prayer or otherwise, Rebbetzin Batya valued dearly the gift of speech. She handled every utterance with sacred and meticulous care, knowing well that the spoken word does not really dissolve into air. She understood that Hashem listens and records.

❧ ❧ ❧

No Tears on Shabbos

AN IMPORTANT GUEST WAS DUE TO ARRIVE. Rebbetzin Batya rejoiced in the prospect. There was much excitement in the anticipation of the visit. As early as Sunday morning she began to tidy her apartment and plan tasty dishes even though the distinguished guest was not expected before sunset the following Friday afternoon. In appreciation of the privilege, no effort was too difficult and no expense too great, even if it meant skimping all week long.

As much as Rebbetzin Batya was anxious to please her guest, she had no intention of spending beyond her means. She was not one to entertain lavishly on credit. At the same time, she did not seek special bargains in order to stretch her money. She considered the acquisition of *mitzvos* to be the best bargain available and looked for them in every purchase she made. She went, for example, to great pains to find a grocery store operated by a poor widow and enjoyed paying for what she bought. Indeed, she was so anxious to help a poor person earn a living that, regardless of the inconvenience, she often went out of her neighborhood to buy groceries. This self-imposed hardship may have seemed unreasonable, especially since her shopping budget amounted to an insignificant sum. She, however, knew better. She knew that in the eyes of Hashem the pennies spent on a *mitzvah* were precious.

Her shopping skill was admired. Even fruit and vegetable vendors were touched by the gentle treatment Rebbetzin Batya gave their produce. She was one of the few who was not wont to upset their stalls, fishing and groping for choice merchandise. On the contrary, she was more concerned about the produce she left behind than with what she carried home. And yet as much as Rebbetzin Batya preferred to be the loser, there seemed to be *brachah* and sweetness in what she bought. What's more, this was more likely to delight her distinguished guest than pomposity.

Early Friday morning Rebbetzin Batya hurried to Rav Tarfon Street in the center of Bnei Brak to buy a live chicken. Because she wanted the meat to be especially fresh for the occasion she left this chore for Friday. On the spot, she had a reliable *shochet* slaughter the chicken. There was still lots to do before the chicken was ready to be served. Even before the involved koshering process, Rebbetzin Batya examined the chicken inside and out for possible blemishes. She gave the lungs and gizzard special attention. Had they been punctured for some reason, the chicken would not have been fit. Time was of the essence but Rebbetzin Batya patiently and deliberately inspected everything to the last detail. She was guided by the law and nothing was overlooked. As always, there was help from Above, and regardless of possible last-minute complications, the preparations were completed in due time.

As the sun readied to set Friday afternoon, the little home sparkled. The table was beautifully set and Rebbetzin Batya's heart filled with festive joy. There was unusual grace in the way she lit her candles and prayed:

"Blessed art Thou Hashem, our G-d, King of the Universe Who has sanctified us by Thy commandments and commanded us to kindle the Shabbos light."

The guest, the "Shabbos Queen," had at last arrived. Now all of Rebbetzin Batya's hard work was behind her, and the entertaining began in earnest. She welcomed her Shabbos with genuine warmth: "What can I do for you, Shabbos Queen? What more can I do?" she wanted to know. She simply could not exert herself enough on behalf of the holy day, her special guest.

It was on such a Shabbos in 1953 that the Chazon Ish suddenly departed this life. The news spread rapidly. Bnei Brak was blanketed by heavy sadness. People mourned the loss not only of a revered sage but, even more so, of a devoted father.

The moving force behind the Chazon Ish's selfless dedication to his people — only recently illustrated by his fight against compulsory army service for girls — had been a deeply loving heart, a gentle heart that cared. Now that it beat no more, the loss was keenly felt by Torah-observant Jews the world over. Few, however, felt the loss as much as Rebbetzin Batya. Members of the Karelitz family feared her reaction to her brother's passing.

As soon as Rebbetzin Esther (Greineman) Finkel heard the painful news, she rushed to her Aunt Batya's home, wishing to be by her side in this time of sorrow. She worried about her aunt and wondered how her weak heart would withstand the blow.

Esther was more or less unnoticed as she entered her aunt's small sitting room. The scene she witnessed was as unbelievable as it was unforgettable. She stood at the door and watched and listened spellbound.

Rav Nochum Meir sat at the table and his rebbetzin stood facing him. It was obvious that she was tense and her control forced as she begged her husband: "Please tell me, tell me . . ." She seemed to want the answer in a hurry. "Tell me, what does the Talmud say? What exactly happens in heaven when a *tzaddik* arrives? Tell me about the welcome he gets. Tell me all about the many angels who rejoice and rush to meet him. What about the *tzaddikim*, his mother and father? When do they greet him? Tell me about the happy day in heaven!"

It was obvious that the tears were choked up in her throat but Rebbetzin Batya had important company. Not for one moment had she forgotten her guest, the Shabbos Queen. It simply was not proper to sadden the Shabbos.

Rav Nochum Meir was deeply grieved as well. He had lost not only a brother-in-law but also a close friend, guide and teacher. Indeed, the close relationship of mutual respect the two *gedolim* had enjoyed was rare. And yet, regardless of personal feelings, Rav Nochum Meir was anxious to oblige. He kept his rebbetzin captivated with fascinating descriptions of life beyond death.

Rav Nochum Meir knew Rebbetzin Batya's ways very well. Still, she never failed to surprise him. She managed it without exerting herself in any way. On that fateful Shabbos, Rav Nachum Meir and Esther were moved by her unexpected spiritual strength. For not until the Shabbos was escorted out in dignity and the *havdalah* prayer recited did she release her tears. She then wept bitterly for a long time.

CHAPTER THIRTEEN

True Love

TIMES OF RELATIVE PEACE followed the War of Independence. The Jewish nation was given a chance to catch its breath. Every segment of the community rushed to make the best

Happy Days of the situation. There was an acute sense of urgency in the common effort of revitalization and rebuilding.

The Zionists in the newborn state feverishly engaged in promoting and establishing *kibbutzim* and developing the cities and towns. The pioneering spirit, which dominated the growth of the country, entailed considerable hardship. This tended to preclude rapid and qualitative family growth. There was also a feeling that it was unfair and irresponsible to expose too many children to the rigors of a life style to which much of the populace had become accustomed and committed.

In sharp contrast, the Torah-observant community multiplied spiritually and physically. In response to the first Torah commandment — to be fruitful and multiply — religious life, as always, focused on building the family. The proliferation of children was viewed as a blessing that enriched the family, the community and all of *Klal Yisrael.* Consequently, Rebbetzin Batya was kept busy with joyous occasions. Wedding followed wedding. Batsheva married Rav Avraham Schwartz. Shoshana, too, married a Ponevez alumnus, Rav Zelig Privalsky. Rav Nissim stood under the *chupah* with Leah Kopfshitz, and Yehoshua Tanchum married Leah's cousin, Miriam Sheinker. Nephews and nieces followed suit. Esther Greineman married Rav Beinish Finkel, who later became *Rosh Yeshiva* of Mir in Jerusalem, and the Steipler Gaon's only son, Rav Chaim Kanievsky, married Batsheva Elyashiv, a daughter of the prominent Torah scholar and *posek*, Rav Shlomo Elyashiv, and a granddaughter of the renowned *tzaddik*, Rav Aryeh Levin. Indeed, without exception, all who joined Rebbetzin Batya's family were Jewish royalty, the cream of Orthodoxy.

In the wake of these unions an abundance of grandchildren, grandnephews and nieces was not long in coming. The family experienced repeated blessings of fruitfulness. It almost seemed as if the many departed souls that had risen during the horror of Nazi Germany were now vying with one another to reenter the earthly world. Every newborn baby was living and dramatic proof of the continuity and indeed the eternity of the Jewish people, rendering every birth doubly precious. This was a time of renaissance and regeneration.

In the Torah-observant community there was, in this time of economic austerity, a deep and abiding faith that G-d in his everlasting bounty would provide and that the land of milk and honey would sustain her children as their need required. As with mother's milk, production would become commensurate with demand, and the earth would yield its produce accordingly. If the absence of the Children of Israel for nearly two millennia had caused the earth to withhold its fruit, their return to the land would enable it to sprout in abundance and to flower. The religious community as a whole and Rebbetzin Batya's family in particular dedicated themselves to prove worthy of these blessings by demonstrating ceaseless faith in their Provider.

The 1950's became the fullest and happiest period in the lives of Rebbetzin Batya and Rav Nochum Meir. They were continuously surrounded by sweet little children who filled their days with endless joy. Every *bris milah*, every first haircutting that left a three-year-old with *payos*, every first day of *cheder* or Bais

Yaakov marked a memorable milestone not only in the lives of the youngsters but in the lives of their grandparents as well.

Long before his grandchildren were born, Rav Nochum Meir had prepared for their coming. He had exerted every effort to insure that Jewish children would be provided the finest in religious education. He had been instrumental in founding *Chinuch Atzmai* and was active in the supervision of its curriculum. His counsel was sought often on various matters of Torah education.

"What should we stress in a little girl's textbook?" was a question once put to Rav Nochum Meir by a group of teachers who frequented his home. "Stress compassion, and seek to inject into the child a feeling of *hakaras hatov* — a sense of gratitude and appreciation," he advised. To illustrate, he told the following story:

"The weather was stormy. The rain came down in torrents. A small, shivering and soaked bird perched on the window sill. It cried, '*Tzif, tzif* . . . Help me, please!'

"Little Chana rushed to the window. She felt sorry for the helpless bird. She gently opened the window and somehow managed to bring the bird inside. She dried its wings and fed it crumbs of bread. The little bird said, '*Tzif* . . . *Tzif* . . . Thank you, Chana. Thank you!'

"When the rain stopped and the sun shone again, Chana opened the window and allowed the bird to fly off. But soon it returned, perched again briefly on the window sill and said happily, '*Tzif* . . . *Tzif* . . . Thank you, Chana. Thank you!' "

The story, eloquent in its simplicity, suggested to the child — in terms she could understand — an element of compassion, the desire to alleviate distress, and a sense of gratitude for a kindness conferred. The teachers liked it, and it later appeared in a textbook.

Rebbetzin Batya took an interest in all the meetings Rav Nochum Meir conducted in their home. She nevertheless preferred to be a bystander and listen to the goings-on in characteristic silence. Perhaps because she never had an urge to prove herself, she had full confidence in her husband's ability to handle his affairs. From time to time opportunities did present themselves for her talents to find expression. Occasionally, when least expected, the depth of her thoughts and feelings managed to surface.

🦋 🦋 🦋

On her ninth birthday, Esther Greineman was presented with a small diary. She ran at once to show it to her aunt. She begged her to write something in the new and beckoning journal.

"Of course!" Rebbetzin Batya replied good-naturedly, and, taking the diary in hand, began to inscribe her entry. In a few minutes she composed a poem in Yiddish, perfect in rhyme and rhythm. The poem began, "Esther!" Its theme was the significance of the name Esther, which embodied the finest traits of Jewish royalty and Jewish responsibility. It described Queen Esther's sacrificial loyalty to her people and ended with a wish that little Esther emulate her namesake.

As Esther Greineman matured in years, the diary increasingly acquired a value over and above sentiment. Even when she herself became Grandma Finkel, she cherished the book as a constant reminder of her tie to Tante Bashl and the indelible lesson which her poem contained. She was later to gain prominence as Rebbetzin Finkel among a wide circle of Jews, who were convinced that she had done justice to the name Esther. Surely Tante Bashl's influence had left its mark.

Most gratifying to Rebbetzin Batya, however, was her eldest granddaughter Tzipora's promising writing talent. Tzipora Rosenberg is a gifted writer of children's story books and has compiled educational material for use in the Bais Yaakov schools. Much of what she wrote was inspired by her grandmother to whom she was a great source of *nachas*.

One of Rebbetzin Batya's last requests was that Tzipora write something for public dissemination to promote feminine modesty. She even offered to pay the costs involved. Tzipora of course complied and published a little pamphlet that more or less read as follows:

"It is hot! A time for leisure and ice cream! But do you still watch the length of your sleeves? Do they cover the elbow?"

The style reflected well Rebbetzin Batya's ways — a firm message combined with a gentle approach.

⚘   ⚘   ⚘

TOWARD THE END OF THE 1950's Rav Nochum Meir fell gravely ill. The doctors were at a loss to determine the cause of his

The Depth of a Sigh condition. He traveled to the United States to seek more advanced medical aid. There he received excellent care and attention, but no cure. One pleasant occurrence on the trip was a meeting with his closest boyhood friend and his *chavrusa* of many years, Rav Aharon Kotler, the revered and distinguished *Rosh Yeshivah* of Lakewood.

Upon returning to Israel, Rav Nochum Meir was increasingly confined to bed. His pain increased in intensity as the treatment received became less and less effective. Rebbetzin Batya did everything she could to diminish his suffering. He responded by doing everything possible to spare her anxiety and worry. He exercised such control that not even a sigh was allowed to escape from him in her presence. Unfortunately it was not always possible for him to sense her nearness. Occasionally she walked into the bedroom unnoticed by him. Once, when Rav Nochum Meir had uttered a deep sigh, his wife rushed to his side to offer assistance. He did his best to put her at ease.

"It is nothing, really nothing," he said smiling faintly. "Do you know what a miraculous pain-reliever a sigh can be? Do you know what a gracious present from Heaven a sigh is?" Then he went on at length to explain the miraculous effect of a simple sigh. To his friends, however, he confided that the pains he suffered were at times unbearable.

Rav Nochum Meir's suffering evoked the memory of Rabbi Chanina Ben Tradyon. The *Gemara* relates that Rabbi Chanina was one of the ten holy martyrs tortured to death by the Romans. After the Romans wrapped Rabbi Chanina's body in a Torah scroll, the parchment was set ablaze. At the same time, they placed

Rav Nochum Meir Karelitz in his old age

layers of wet wool on Rabbi Chanina's chest in order to prolong his agony. Some of his devoted students stood by helplessly witnessing their revered teacher being burned alive. Aware that the saintly are endowed with prophetic vision shortly before death, one student mustered enough courage to approach Rabbi Chanina and ask with trepidation, "What do you see, Rabbi?"

In the very tempest of his ordeal Rabbi Chanina managed a reply: "I see the golden letters of the Torah rising heavenward in the flames. Only the parchment is being consumed by the fire. The letters are eternal" (*Avodah Zarah*, pages 17, 18).

A measure of the same quality was perceived in Rav Nochum Meir. Only his body was consumed by the dreaded disease. The spirit and the Torah within him rose heavenward in eternity.

❈ ❈ ❈

Rebbetzin Batya deeply mourned the loss of her husband. But she did not wail and weep for all to see. She did not seek sympathy and did not feel sorry for herself. Instead, she continued to serve her husband by keeping alive his memory.

When her grandchildren grew in understanding, she told them of Rav Nochum Meir's peaceful, unassuming manner. She told them of his boundless love for Torah and his compassion for people, of the sacred value of his word, how much he had honored and dignified every human being with whom he had been in contact, how he had guided the ignorant and had sought to mend the ways of those who had gone astray. She also remembered to tell them of how much depth there was in a simple sigh.

🦋 🦋 🦋

The Esrog and the Silver Box

FOR YEARS REBBETZIN BATYA'S younger daughter-in-law, Rebbetzin Miriam, had been bent on surprising her husband, Rav Yehoshua Tanchum, with a sterling-silver esrog box. For years she had saved pennies until she was able to purchase one. Now she rushed to show it to her mother-in-law. A bit nervously, she unwrapped her package and waited for her reaction. The box was indeed beautiful.

The rebbetzin examined the box with unexpected solemnity. She looked and examined it for some time, as if counting in her mind the many pennies and weighing the sacrifice that had gone into its acquisition. Then in a soft tone of voice she said, "One should save to buy the most kosher and beautiful esrog."

No doubt the rebbetzin had considered her daughter-in-law's feelings before offering her opinion. No doubt she would have liked nothing better than to compliment her on her good taste and thoughtful gesture. After all, it was her son that her daughter-in-law had wished to please. Yet she voiced her conviction in as blunt a way as she could because personal considerations were of secondary importance. Her view on the silver box was basic to her faith, and she wanted Rebbetzin Miriam to know wherein Jewish priorities lay. She wanted her to know what had real and lasting value and what was worthy of sacrifice.

In terms of economics the sterling-silver box was an excellent and lasting investment. The esrog, on the other hand, was a perishable fruit with a value that could not survive the Succos Yom

Tov. But Rebbetzin Batya knew better. She knew that the *mitzvah* inherent in the sacrificial buying of a kosher and beautiful *esrog* had everlasting value. Faith demonstrated in the obedience to Hashem's commandment was priceless.

As a rule, Rebbetzin Batya never lost an opportunity to direct one's eyes inward. To her, the container's content was more important than the container itself. In the same vein, when on *Simchas Torah* eve she witnessed from the *ezras nashim* of Kollel Chazon Ish the many men and children dancing enthusiastically with the *sifrei Torah*, she remarked: "Some of the men hug the *sefer Torah* with burning love." To her, this affection and reverence for Torah mirrored true dedication to the written word within Torah. In sharp contrast, of course, are those who are impressed with the heavy, antique, silver crowns that adorn the Torah while ignoring and transgressing the holy teachings within.

Rebbetzin Miriam loved her mother-in-law dearly and valued her tutelage. Her respect and high regard for her were evident years later when she related this experience involving the silver *esrog* box. It was one of the more meaningful lessons she had learned from Rebbetzin Batya.

❀   ❀   ❀

THE PATTERN OF REBBETZIN BATYA'S LIFE closely resembled that of her mother. It would be difficult to find two lives more parallel.

Is It too Much to Ask? Both women were totally devoted to Torah from early childhood to the very end of a ninety-year life span. Both enjoyed longevity in the face of continuous physical weakness. Tragedy too struck at about the same age. Both were widowed at seventy. During their long widowhood of twenty years, they both saw their aspirations fulfilled. Both were catered to by their children with rare respect and devotion. But in spite of the similarities, there was one marked difference in the way Heaven had managed their lives. Rebbetzin Batya, more than her mother, was constantly tested. Her life was one long trial.

In her early eighties, when Rebbetzin Batya had well earned

peaceful retirement, when she might have sat back and enjoyed the fruits of her long labor, she was tried more than ever before.

※ ※ ※

In the city of Bnei Brak and beyond, Rebbetzin Batya's two sons were well known. Rav Nissim, the older of the two, had been drawn early into public service by the community even though he would have preferred to continue learning undisturbed in Kollel Chazon Ish. His younger brother, Rav Yehoshua Tanchum, however, managed to do just that. And yet as much as Rav Yehoshua Tanchum sought to hide from the public eye, he was nevertheless noticed and esteemed. Whenever he entered Kollel Chazon Ish or Kollel Ponevez, the *avreichim* rose from their seats in respect. This attention pained him considerably. At the end of a day's learning, he would often return home upset. Rebbetzin Miriam knew why.

"Why, why do they do it?" he would ask, annoyed. He simply detested the attention. In all his life, only once did Rav Yehoshua Tanchum express a desire to be honored. That was on the day when Reb Nochum Mendel Sheinin, a legendary figure, humble and pious, had died.

Almost all of Bnei Brak, including Rav Yehoshua Tanchum and his wife Miriam, attended the funeral. To everyone's surprise, no eulogies were delivered. Reb Mendel in his last testament had strictly forbidden any praise or mention of him.

Like everyone else, Rebbetzin Miriam expressed disappointment as she complained to her husband, "I missed the *hespeidim*. What a shame! The life of a man so righteous as Reb Mendel serves as a lesson to all and his eulogy is of benefit to the living. We need the *mussar!*"

Rav Yehoshua Tanchum reacted with gravity. "If only I could benefit my people," he said, "I would readily allow eulogies of myself."

Several weeks later, at ten o'clock on a Friday morning, Rav Yehoshua Tanchum suffered a fatal accident. He was rushed unconscious to Tel Hashomer Hospital. Rebbetzin Miriam had

Rav Nissim   *Rav Yehoshua Tanchum צ״ל*

witnessed the accident. She too was taken to the hospital in a state of shock.

News of the tragedy spread like wildfire through the observant community. All of Bnei Brak prayed for mercy from the All Merciful. Many stood vigil at the hospital waiting for a miracle to occur. The doctors worked around the clock in an effort to revive a body that was already medically gone. Their feverish activity was encouraged by the supernatural state that appeared to exist. They did not know what kept the body alive.

Upon hearing the news, Rebbetzin Esther Finkel rushed from Jerusalem to Bnei Brak. She by-passed the hospital. Her thoughts were with her Tante Bashl. She feared, lest in all the anguished turmoil, Rebbetzin Batya might be forgotten and left to bear the agonizing news alone at home. Rebbetzin Esther wished to be at her aunt's side at such a time.

As she had suspected, Rebbetzin Finkel found her aunt at home alone. She was a broken woman. Yet she managed to address

Esther with compassion and feeling. "It is good you came," she said appreciatively. "Yes, it is good you came." Then with a tremor in her voice came a heart-rending question: "Tell me, please! Tell me. Is it too much to ask that Hashem return a father to his children and a husband to his wife? Is it too much to ask?"

In her concern for others she failed to ask Hashem to return a son to his mother.

Just before sunset on Sunday, the eve of the 15th day of Cheshvan, 1976, Rebbetzin Batya lit a *yahrzeit* candle in memory of the Chazon Ish. No sooner had she done this than in walked Dr. Moshe Rothschild, who gave her the news that her son had departed from this world. He had never regained consciousness. On Monday, Bnei Brak witnessed one of the biggest funerals in its history. *Hespeidim* were delivered throughout the day for both the Chazon Ish and his nephew, Rav Yehoshua Tanchum. It was a day of grief and deep mourning for all of Bnei Brak.

During the seven days of *shivah*, the stream of people who came to offer condolences was endless. The sorrow shared with the bereaved was genuine and deep. All came to express their feelings of sincere sympathy, but Rebbetzin Batya invited only silence. For seven long days she sat on her little stool without uttering a word.

At a time of misfortune, speech tends to mitigate pain. The broken heart yearns to cry out and complain. Perhaps precisely because of this, Rebbetzin Batya refrained from speaking. To her, speech was dangerous lest she utter a word that may be construed as rebellious to the Almighty, or be deemed something other than complete and unsullied submission to the will of G-d. She well knew that "Hashem gives and Hashem takes" (*Job* 1:21). Her total acceptance of His inscrutable will, reflected in her attitude and demeanor, were summed up in the perennial blessing recited on hearing news of death: "*Baruch Dayan HaEmes* (Blessed be the true Judge)."

Rebbetzin Batya's silence was seen as unusual strength, conviction and resolve. The unspoken word was a lesson to many. At the same time, silence provided an opportunity to think and recollect. This was a time to relive the many experiences she had shared with her wonderful son. The cold Chanukah night — when she carried Yehoshua Tanchum within her and slipped into an icy ditch from which she had extricated herself with difficulty — came to mind. She recalled how she had prayed for a Chanukah miracle to occur and how speedily she had been answered. It became clear to her that she ought to be thankful for all the precious years she had been fortunate to have a son like Yehoshua Tanchum. In the midst of sorrow she found reason to be grateful. This was because she knew well what life and death were all about. She knew that one may gain eternity in a split second while others may waste away in longevity. She knew that there are those who live after death, and there are those who are dead while they live. The length of time spent on earth was indeed irrelevant.

When she recalled Yehoshua Tanchum's *bris milah*, she remembered all the guests who had come from Vilna for the occasion. The Chazon Ish was among those who had made the trip, and she had been thrilled with his presence at the *simchah*. Now again it was fitting that on the anniversary of his own death the Chazon Ish escort his nephew on High.

Certainly Rav Nochum Meir's many beautiful stories of life beyond this life were still vivid in her memory. She had more than sufficient enriching thoughts to keep her mind active during the seven days. She managed well without speech.

Some time after she rose from the *shivah*, she did, however, express her feelings to those close to her. "I know, I know," she said with certainty, "that Yehoshua Tanchum is in good company. He lives in splendor surrounded by great *tzaddikim*: his father, grandparents, uncles, the Chazon Ish and a host of sages." But then she added longingly, "I would just like to know what he does. I would like to see what he does."

This wish was understandable. She was the kind of mother who had always known what her children were doing.

CHAPTER FOURTEEN
Charming Dignity

FOLLOWING THE TRAGIC PASSING of Rav Yehoshua Tanchum, the first joyous occasion within the Karelitz family was the engagement of Rav Nissim's daughter Sara to American-born, **Life with** Ponevez-educated Oren Austern, the grandson of **Royalty** Reb Elkana Austern. The *shidduch* had been promoted by the *Rosh Yeshivah* of Ponevez, Harav Eliezer Menachem Man Shach.

The Austerns lived in a spacious, nine-room villa in fashionable Savyon. Here Oren and Sara were to celebrate their *tena'im*. At the end of summer in 1977, Esther, Oren's mother, commenced preparations for the occasion. She was ill at ease. She had reservations about hosting the Karelitz family. They were recognized as aristocracy. At the same time they were extremely poor. She was neither.

When expecting company generally, Esther was in the habit of starting preparations early. She polished all her silver and furniture. She made sure to find an appropriate place for each and every knickknack she owned. Everything of value had to be on display. The carpeting was vacuumed and checked for stains. Stubborn stains were hidden by covering them with furniture. When all was set and ready, Esther ran through the house nervously. With a critical eye, she reexamined the looks of things.

To her dismay she discovered that her spacious living room was not impressive enough. Several noticeable blemishes were downright shameful. One lamp shade, for example, had been badly faded by the sun, and two walls appeared bare without the fine paintings she would have liked to have had hanging. She would also have liked to increase the size of the room by placing a large mirror on the wall above the black marble fireplace — if only she had some extra funds.

Hosting the Karelitz family, however, posed a dilemma of a different nature. All of a sudden the Austern home seemed more of a mansion. This time Esther was not anxious to exhibit wealth beyond her means. On the contrary, she was concerned about her guests' reaction to a kind of affluence that had not been theirs. There was also the possibility of a reverse snobbishness, a belittling attitude on their part to her materialistic life style.

Esther thereupon rushed to conceal all her silver, knickknacks, mirrors and paintings. Everything showy was out of sight. The duller the look the better she liked it. Regretfully she had no way of hiding the baby-grand piano, and she could not roll up the wall-to-wall carpeting. The sunken living-room floor could not be raised, and there was no way to hide the two French provincial love seats, the blue-velvet upholstered couch, the coffee and end tables, etc. . . . etc. . . . Never before had Esther felt so loaded with possessions. Never before had she a greater desire for simplicity. Little did she realize then that her preparations in the service of the Karelitz family were leading her in a right and proper direction.

The *kallah* and her entire family, including her two grandmothers, Rebbetzin Batya and Rebbetzin Chaya Kopfshitz, arrived. Esther welcomed them cordially and scrutinized them. This was her opportunity to meet and study the ways of the Karelitz family. The first impression she was to gain was important to her. By the time the women had taken their seats in the living room and the men had crowded into the dining room, Esther had formed a fairly accurate picture of the *kallah's* background. This indeed was Jewish aristocracy.

In a most natural way, without being stiff or pretentious, all sat quietly and conversed sparingly. There was unusual grace and dignity about them. Although everything their eyes saw was novel to them, no one gaped in astonishment, no one took inventory. Nor did anyone look down condescendingly upon luxury. They simply did not relate to the surroundings. It was as if they had entered a playroom filled with expensive toys. Of course it was expected of children to be entertained by toys, but they were adults.

Rebbetzin Batya sat on the couch with the *kallah* by her side. Sara was a bit nervous during the course of the evening. The proximity of her grandmother calmed her. Rebbetzin Batya smiled sweetly and reacted with warmth when addressed. Otherwise she appeared to be in deep thought throughout the evening. Rebbetzin Chaya, on the other hand, had a joyous glow all about her. It was a *Yiddishe simchah*, a great event, and she was delighted with the blessing. Yet the general mood was one of subdued festivity. The loud and lively chatter common to social gatherings was missing. These women were careful to avoid it.

Esther was curious to know Rebbetzin Batya's thoughts. What were they? She was solemn but not sad or troubled. What then occupied her thoughts?

When Esther later came to know the rebbetzin more intimately, she received the answer she had sought: At her granddaughter Sarah's *tena'im*, Rebbetzin Batya marveled at the strength of Torah. That Torah stood a chance to flourish with such intensity in the heart of Savyon's secular world moved her. She admired the young men of this household who were ready and willing to part with tempting comforts in order to learn Torah full time. Because she had lived a life of struggle and privation, she valued the sacrifice. In short, she found *ruchnius* in Savyon.

"WHEN THE MONTH OF ADAR ENTERS, we increase our happiness" (*Ta'anis* 29). Oren and Sara were married in the month of Adar,

A Pertinent Question

1978. From that time on, Esther was to visit Rebbetzin Batya often. She considered every meeting with the valiant lady a privilege and a unique experience.

On one such occasion Esther found Rebbetzin Batya in her tiny reception room. She sat at the table with an open book of *Tehillim* in front of her. In the center of the covered table was a bowl filled with tangerines and nuts.

"I hope I am not intruding," Esther said apologetically, as she stood in the doorway about to enter.

"Come in, please. Come in and take a seat," Rebbetzin Batya begged. "It is nice of you to come." The sincere invitation led Esther to believe that she was an important guest. "Surely you are no bother," she continued. "I have all day to say *Tehillim*."

As soon as Esther sat down, Rebbetzin Batya offered her some fruit, saying, "Please make a *brachah*." Esther obeyed. She took a tangerine and in an audible voice recited the blessing over the fruit. This enabled the rebbetzin to answer *amen*. She appreciated this opportunity. She knew the value and meaning of every *amen* she uttered. Esther was still in the midst of eating the tangerine when Rebbetzin Batya remarked with admiration, "Your son is a very fine young man." She paused for a minute or two and then added: "Yes, your son knows how to organize time. He knows the full value of time."

Appreciating the compliment, Esther rushed to reciprocate and said, "I like Sara. She is an exceptionally fine girl."

Here was an opportunity for the rebbetzin to elaborate on the background her granddaughter enjoyed, a good time to praise her family's *yichus*. But it was not her way. Instead, she simply asked a pertinent question, "How do you know that Sara is fine when she hardly ever talks?"

Esther understood the intimation. It was clear that the rebbetzin was familiar with the times she lived in. She knew that in her day and age demagoguery, cheap advertising, blasphemy and tongue-lashing were the tools of aggrandizement. In a time when it is common practice for one to boast of being greater, smarter and more qualified than others, Rebbetzin Batya wondered how Esther was able to appreciate a refinement disciplined by silence.

❀　❀　❀

IN 1979 THE MONTH OF ADAR again brought good tidings. Sara Austern gave birth to an anxiously awaited baby boy. The news

The Bris Milah thrilled and invigorated the entire Karelitz family. This baby meant a great deal to Rebbetzin Batya. He was a very special gift.

On the day of the *bris milah*, the family and friends gathered at the Sanz Synagogue in Bnei Brak to celebrate the occasion. Rebbetzin Batya was *kvatterin*, the woman who brings the baby into the room where the *bris milah* is performed. In a small room adjacent to the *shul*, Sara dressed her baby in an all-white ensemble and crowned his tiny head with a white *yarmulke* she had sewn. Then she placed a firm, king-size pillow into a white-on-white embroidered pillowcase and gently placed her baby upon it. She lifted the pillow with her baby on it and lovingly handed it to her grandmother. The scene was touching. All eyes were on the rebbetzin as she carried the baby into the synagogue for his circumcision. Rebbetzin Batya was not aware of the many people about her. She seemed to be in deep thought as she gazed into distant space. There was a visible glow on her face. She was elated. A highlight of the solemn ceremony was reached when she heard the baby's name, Yehoshua Tanchum, announced for the first time. This meaningful moment was her beautiful sunrise after her sun had set.

Solemnity gave way to joy. The guests were invited to partake of the *seudas mitzvah*. The baby's two grandmothers, Rebbetzin Leah and Esther, sat side by side at a table bedecked with delicious food and drink, all prepared by various members of the Karelitz family. After Esther thanked Rebbetzin Leah and the others for the tasty dishes served so graciously, she remarked, "The baby looks angelic with the white *yarmulke* on his little head. I don't recall ever seeing a skullcap on a baby's head at his *bris*."

Rebbetzin Leah smiled with pride and said: "This is an old and sacred Karelitz tradition. The Chazon Ish attached great importance to the custom. He often reiterated that the *yarmulke* was a *segulah* for *yiras shamayim*. All the Karelitz boys have worn skullcaps from the time of their *bris*."

After giving the matter some thought, Esther marveled: "Perhaps more than ever before the skullcap has become a symbol of *Yiddishkeit*. It is a kind of uniform. No matter the size, shape, material or the color, it is worn with pride and *yiras shamayim*."

In the midst of her spirited mood, Esther observed Rebbetzin Batya. At all occasions, in every situation, she was an inspiration. Even now as she sat at the *seudas mitzvah*, there was dignity and a quiet air of contentment about her.

Esther felt good about the *yarmulke* her new baby grandson wore at his *bris*. She was more than happy to be in partnership with the Karelitz family. The precious new addition to her family was her royal connection.

❀ ❀ ❀

REBBETZIN LEAH SPENT MUCH TIME with her mother-in-law. She would often leave her apartment in the middle of household

A Single Match chores and walk down a flight of stairs to see if Rebbetzin Batya needed her. It was therefore not unusual for Esther to meet her whenever she dropped in to visit. Esther regarded the opportunity a privilege and an uplifting experience. She admired and respected the ways of them both.

Rebbetzin Leah's quiet and calm disposition is inborn and her deep-rooted piety is due to the finest of Jewish rearing. She is the daughter of Rav Zvi Kopfshitz, the granddaughter of Rav Shmuel Hillel Sheinker and great-granddaughter of Rav Yosef Chaim Sonnenfeld. That she had had the added *zechus* to live many years in the proximity of Rebbetzin Batya was evident from an experience Rebbetzin Leah related to Esther.

"Soon after the Rav arrived home from the *beis din*,* I prepared his supper for him and cooked it on a small flame," she began slowly. "Somehow the wind blew out the fire under the pot. When I tried to rekindle the flame, I discovered that the box of matches was empty. I searched for a single match, but there was not one to

---

* *Beis din* is a religious court. Rav Nissim heads one of the two *batei din* in Bnei Brak.

3 generations: Rav Sonnenfeld, his son-in-law Rav Sheinker and Rav Kopfshitz.

be found. As I walked out of the kitchen I noticed a box of matches on the table near the ashtray. My married son had lit a cigarette several hours earlier and had forgotten to take his matches home with him. I must say I was glad. It seemed to me to be a special *mazal*. You know how annoying it is not to find a match when you need it in a hurry?" She paused a bit before continuing. "I took the match box and was about to return to the kitchen when suddenly I switched course and went to see the rav instead. When the rav lifted his head from his *sefer*, I told him of my predicament and asked if I may borrow one match from my son's box of matches. I of course expected to buy matches first thing in the morning and return the borrowed match.

"The rav stated the law plainly: 'You may not borrow anything — not even a match — without the rightful owner's knowledge and permission.'

"Can you imagine how close I was to transgressing the law?" Rebbetzin Leah asked and then added, "It is frightening! Look how careful we must be not to err."

"It is not likely that you, Rebbetzin Leah, would, G-d forbid, err," Esther assured her. "An experienced driver knows when to slam on the brakes. As for myself, I would never have even posed the question. It would never have occurred to me that a predicament existed. My reasoning would have permitted me to borrow the match without qualms. It is of course wrong that I take the law into my own hands."

Rebbetzin Leah's instincts and reflexes were sharp and alert, because she had the *zechus* to have observed Rebbetzin Batya from close range. To find questions in need of answers was her mother-in-law's specialty, as was the lesson that even a well-known *posek's* wife needs sometimes to ask questions.

CHAPTER FIFTEEN
Boundless Room in a Weak Heart

N 1980 SARA AND OREN moved into their own two-bedroom, 720-square-foot apartment on Sorotzkin Street in Bnei Brak. The bedrooms in the apartment were so small that no

The Apartment matter how the beds were arranged access to the closet was blocked. To get to and open the closet door, at least one bed had to be pushed to an angle. The tiny kitchen did have two sinks, one for dairy and one for meat, but not enough cabinet space to hold two sets of dishes. Nevertheless, the occasion of moving into the new home was celebrated on the fourteenth day of Adar in a grand way. Sara invited her parents, brothers and sisters and, of course, her two grandmothers to a festive Purim *seudah*.

For several months thereafter, Esther hesitated to visit Rebbetzin Batya. Esther feared that she might criticize her judgment and lack of foresight in buying her granddaughter an apartment that was outgrown even before it was occupied. Was it not expected of a Savyonite to be a bit more generous?

In time Esther mustered the courage to drive to Bnei Brak and pay the rebbetzin a visit. She intended to plead her case by describing the dire financial situation her family was in. She planned to explain how most of the family's wealth and livelihood had been lost; how nine apartment houses in the Bronx section of

New York City had to be abandoned because landlords in New York were at the mercy of their tenants, a hostile court and the media; how it was impossible to maintain buildings when tenants had a vested right to harass owners to a point where their reputation and very life were in danger. In short, Esther wanted Rebbetzin Batya to know how this injustice had drained her family of all their savings and forced them to sell their home in Savyon.

On the way to Bnei Brak, Esther reviewed her thoughts over and over in the hope of soliciting and gaining understanding and perhaps sympathy. What Rebbetzin Batya thought of her and her family was important to Esther.

The warm reception Esther received the minute she entered the apartment put her immediately at ease. She felt as if she had been expected for some time. Now that she had arrived, Rebbetzin Batya was delighted to see her. Esther had hardly sat down when in a sweet tone of voice she said, "*A za shaineh shtub! A za shaineh dirah!* (Such a beautiful home! Such a beautiful apartment!)"

There was genuine gratitude in the two short sentences. Esther said not a word. She was stunned by this sincere desire to express thanks. She was also amazed by the speed with which Rebbetzin Batya had rushed to acknowledge a kind act. It was obvious that *hakaras hatov* was deeply ingrained in her being.

Upon reflection, Esther could not understand how she ever expected Rebbetzin Batya to react differently. It was obvious that this lady of valor could never have followed any other course. Certainly the rebbetzin did not measure the value of a home by the size or number of its rooms. She was not impressed with the number of meters an apartment contained. To her it was only the apartment's occupants that counted. The true measure of its beauty lay in the degree of holiness and purity imparted to their home.

This experience taught Esther a lesson in respect. She realized that she had a distance to go before she could fully understand and appreciate the spiritual level Rebbetzin Batya enjoyed.

IN WALKED REBBETZIN BATYA'S next-door neighbor, old friend and distant relative. She had an urgent plea on her mind. "I simply

The Silence Hurt

cannot take it any longer!" the friend complained nervously. She had good reason to be indignant. The apartment adjacent to her home was being converted into a *shtiebel*. As a result, the racket caused by the tearing down of walls and the blasting of concrete floors was at times ear splitting. The hammering, banging, clatter and shouts of the workers were continuous from early morning until five o'clock in the afternoon. The feverish work went on nonstop.

"We don't have to suffer this insolence!" the neighbor continued angrily. "Between two and four the country rests. The workers well know the law of the land. They know that the law requires them to be quiet at this designated time of rest. We are entitled to this courtesy. I ask them nicely, I plead with them and I beg, but it does no good. They ignore me. There is but one way I can move these workers to listen. If I ask them to work with restraint because the noise disturbs your rest and peace, they would heed my request and respect your wishes."

"But they do not disturb my rest," Rebbetzin Batya said in all sincerity. Indeed, how could the noise of building a *shtiebel* disturb her peace? Under no circumstances would she interfere with or delay even for one moment the completion of a place of worship.

Soon after the neighbor left, the din from without suddenly stopped. Rebbetzin Batya knew why. Her good friend had obviously not heeded her wishes. She was disturbed and saddened by the quiet. In her heart she bore no resentment. She knew her devoted friend. She knew that her friend's visit and concern had not been motivated by selfish consideration. On the contrary, she had only the rebbetzin's well-being at heart. Still, the silence hurt.

❧ ❧ ❧

ON A RAINY, COLD JANUARY AFTERNOON, Esther found Rebbetzin Batya resting on her narrow studio couch in her reception room. She wore a heavy sweater and was covered with several blankets. The bundling up was necessary to keep the damp chill

The Yemenite Woman

from reaching her bones.

"It sure is nasty out," Esther said after she arrived. "What a downpour! When the sun peeks through the clouds it is a lifesaver. Unfortunately it does not last long."

Rebbetzin Batya smiled but did not elaborate on the weather. She preferred silence. The rain was a blessing from Heaven, a gift to be grateful for. Besides, she welcomed Hashem's ways and was never one to murmur against them. When the conversation veered from her path she changed the subject. *"Vos machen dee kleine?* (How are the little ones?),"* she asked with interest. This was a question she never neglected to ask.

Before Esther had a chance to answer, a middle-aged Yemenite woman walked in. Her wet rubber boots were partially hidden by the many long skirts she was wearing beneath her worn outer coat. A woolen kerchief covered her head up to the eyebrows. After placing her dripping wet umbrella in the corner of the room, she walked over to Rebbetzin Batya, stretched out her right hand, palm up, and with a Yemenite accent said, *"Nu, Rebbetzin!"*

The rebbetzin shook her head in agreement, raised her body slowly, lifted her small pillow from under her head and pulled out a tiny purse from under it.

"She wants alms," Rebbetzin Batya said in Yiddish to keep Esther informed of the goings-on. Then she took a single aluminum penny from her purse and placed it into the Yemenite woman's hand. At the same time, Esther rushed to empty her purse full of change into the woman's palm.

To Esther's astonishment, the woman seemed displeased and troubled. She stood baffled, not knowing what to do. "What *chutzpah*! What nerve! You give a finger and they want the hand!" Esther thought, annoyed and indignant.

But the Yemenite woman did not budge. She kept staring at the hand full of change, as if searching for something of special value.

Suddenly her eyes lit up. She spied the penny Rebbetzin Batya had given her. From the midst of all the change, she selected and separated her penny and slipped the rest of the change indifferently into her pocket. But that one penny she held fast, clutching it inside her fist. Before leaving she looked into the rebbetzin's eyes. The two women had hardly exchanged a word. They seemed to have a silent language of their own. The understanding and compassion with which Rebbetzin Batya hosted her Yemenite guest was something to behold. After Rebbetzin Batya reassuringly smiled at the Yemenite woman, she said, "Shalom, Rebbetzin" and left.

For a while Esther and Rebbetzin Batya reflected on the Yemenite woman's visit. The rebbetzin broke the silence and explained the relationship:

"A long time ago, before this woman was married, she would help me from time to time. Whenever she is in the neighborhood she visits me." Rebbetzin Batya was careful not to call the woman a servant or a Yemenite.

Esther was amazed by the unique relationship the two enjoyed. What did they have in common? Obviously the woman could not have worked for Rebbetzin Batya for any length of time. She had never been in a position to afford help. Only in unusual circumstances, in time of extreme need, would she engage the services of a maid. How then did so lasting a tie develop?

The answer was obvious. The most casual acquaintance of Rebbetzin Batya was left with an indelible impression. Invariably a lasting link developed. Almost everyone who had come in contact with her held fast to the tie. This was so because she had room for everybody in her heart.

❦   ❦   ❦

EARLY ONE MORNING, when Rebbetzin Batya was in her late eighties, Esther arrived at her home in a highly agitated and

Hope and Joy distressed mood. She did not knock or wait on the doorstep to be invited in. The urgency of her visit precluded formalities. It was a matter of life and death.

Esther needed her advice and blessing in a hurry, and she rushed in to see her.

Many women came to Rebbetzin Batya with heavy hearts, and she received them all with motherly concern. Seeing Esther in so troubled a state pained her considerably. She was visibly hurt. There was sorrow in her eyes as she waited silently and anxiously to learn what went wrong.

"My daughter-in-law went into labor during the night," Esther began. "I took her immediately to Laniado Hospital in Natanya. There she gave birth prematurely to twin boys. Both babies were put into incubators and doctors watched over them round the clock. But one was too weak to survive and is no longer with us. The second one is fighting for his life." Esther paused to catch her breath. Rebbetzin Batya listened intently and Esther continued, "The baby is tiny, terribly tiny; he weighs less than two kilo (4.4 pounds) — a lot less. The doctors are not encouraging. 'Time will tell,' 'We must wait and see,' is all I hear. But to us the uncertainty and the long hours of waiting are agony. What should we do? What can we do?"

"We must pray," Rebbetzin Batya said, concerned.

"The Steipler Gaon said that the baby will, *b'ezras Hashem*, grow," Esther added as an afterthought.

"If so, then why do you worry?" Rebbetzin Batya wanted to know. "The Steipler said that the baby will grow. Then, *b'ezras Hashem*, the baby will grow."

Her faith in her brother-in-law's judgment was sacred. She well knew how carefully he weighed every word he uttered. She also knew that a *tzaddik* is not swayed by emotions, wishful thinking or an excess of compassion. He is motivated only by truth. He is given foresight, a vision of truth, because he lives by truth.

Several months later, when the baby was long out of the incubator and had grown nicely, Esther reflected upon her earlier visit to Rebbetzin Batya. Only then did she realize that she had been insensitive and rudely inconsiderate. In fact, she could not understand where she had gotten the audacity to burden the rebbetzin with her personal problems, especially since she had suffered so much misfortune herself. Esther further questioned her right to impose upon Rebbetzin Batya at all hours of day and night in complete disregard of her advanced age, her ill health and her right to peace and quiet. Indeed, was it not time that she be spared the suffering of others? Was it not wrong to cause her extra worry and anxiety? And was it not unfair to expect blessings in return for a lack of consideration?

All these questions bothered Esther. She felt a sense of shame, guilt and regret. With all her heart she wished to apologize and ask to be forgiven. But she was never given that chance. As soon as Rebbetzin Batya learned of the baby's progress, she was so movingly happy that apologies were out of place. Her involvement was so genuine, so matter of fact, that the thought of being taken for granted never occurred to her. Such thoughts had no room in her mind. Her servitude was never a burden; it had become a rewarding duty.

At the same time there were many joyous experiences that came to Rebbetzin Batya. Many were the people who rushed to her with hearts full of good tidings. All who knew her wished to have her present at their *simchah*. She was frail and old. She wore the same outfit to all joyous occasions. Yet when she entered a gathering, people knew that she had arrived. The pleasure of her company was deemed a privilege. How much so was dramatically evident a number of times.

In 1977 Rebbetzin Batya's sister, Tzivia Greineman, departed this life. In the middle of the *shloshim* (mourning period), Rebbetzin Batya's grandnephew, Avraham Yeshayahu Greineman, was married to Shulamit Ben Shlomo. Rebbetzin Batya did not attend the wedding. Soon after the *chupah* ceremony, the young couple got into a taxi and slipped away, leaving their wedding guests behind. As the taxi was speeding towards Rebbetzin Batya's apartment, the *chasan* suddenly spotted his great-aunt, Tante Bashl, on Rabbi Akiva Street. Accompanied by her granddaughter Sara, she was in the midst of her after-dinner walk. The taxi halted in front of Rebbetzin Batya. To her surprise the *chasan* and *kallah*, dressed in their wedding attire, got out of

Rebbetzin Batya in her late eighties at a simchah

the taxi in the middle of the street, ignoring the curious onlookers. They chatted with her for a while and did not return to the wedding hall until they had paid their proper respects and received the rebbetzin's blessings. The *chasan* and *kallah* cherished this short but memorable experience. It was a highlight of their wedding.

Toward the end of her eighty-ninth year, Rebbetzin Batya found it difficult to attend the many *simchos* to which she was invited. Simply getting there was a hardship. Yet people yearned to have her and made all kinds of provisions to accommodate her. Once she was driven by car to the Viznitz wedding hall in Bnei Brak, where women were waiting on the sidewalk for her arrival with a chair at hand. When Rebbetzin Batya slowly stepped out of the car, she was seated in the chair and carried with great care up the flight of stairs into the hall. There she was immediately surrounded by admiring relatives and friends, old and young.

Rebbetzin Batya brought added joy to the joyous and hope to the distressed. This was a significant part of her life's mission, a mission from which she never retired.

❋ ❋ ❋

SOON AFTER THE PESACH HOLIDAYS IN 1984, two months before Rebbetzin Batya's ninetieth birthday, Esther paid her a visit.

Mashiach   "How does Rebbetzin Batya feel today?" Esther wanted to know.

"Weak, very weak. I do not have the strength to do what I used to do," she answered with her usual smile.

By now Esther knew that this was not a frail, old lady's complaint. Rather, it was a kind of apology. Rebbetzin Batya intended to express her regrets. She wanted her visitors to know that if the circumstances had been different she would have been more hospitable.

To start the conversation on a pleasant note, Esther began: "A few weeks ago I ate *shalosh seudos* with the children. Sara served me some of Rebbetzin Batya's gefilte fish. It was delicious."

"I am glad you liked my gefilte fish," the rebbetzin acknowledged, again with a smile.

Ever since her sons had married, she had prepared their Shabbos gefilte fish for them. This was her additional way of honoring the Shabbos and supporting her son's Torah learning. As the family grew and her grandchildren married, she provided them too with gefilte fish for Shabbos. She would buy the fish in quantity, grind it and then prepare it in her unique way. Of late, however, her fingers refused to comply and she could not manage the work involved. Therefore, she asked several granddaughters to assist her while she supervised. She directed them in the art of making gefilte fish from start to finish. "Now, please add a pinch more pepper and salt..." "We need another egg or two." She would advise even while she examined the consistency and flavor of the mixture. Both grandmother and granddaughters looked forward with excitement to this joint venture. Knowing all this, Esther was more than happy to mention her having tasted the rebbetzin's gefilte fish. But Rebbetzin Batya reacted with caution. She seemed to be guarding her speech more than ever before. At an age when women become more talkative, she preferred silence. The weaker she became physically, the more she rose spiritually.

Still Esther wished to cheer her up and said, "We live in special times. Many feel it in their bones. *Mashiach iz baderech.* Yes, *Mashiach* is on the way!"

Rebbetzin Batya's gaze darkened. She reacted with unexpected gravity. "Oh, *a za langeh derech.* Oh, what a long way!" she said with a deep sigh. Her few words pierced the heart. The woes of Jewish suffering throughout the ages seemed to be reflected in her one sentence. At least that was what Esther thought. But she was utterly mistaken. This time she was not grieved by the plight and woes of the Jewish people. It was *Mashiach* she felt for. She was pained by the long years of wandering of *Mashiach*. How could the Jewish people be so callous and insensitive to *Mashiach's* suffering and anguish. *Mashiach* yearns to come. Why do the Jewish people refuse him entry? Where is Jewish hospitality and compassion? How much longer must *Mashiach* remain "*baderech*" before the Jewish people live up to their calling? Rebbetzin Batya wondered.

CHAPTER SIXTEEN

Past, Present and Future All in One

THE WEEKS PRECEDING Rebbetzin Batya's ninetieth birthday were difficult ones. At times she felt as if all her physical strength had left her. This, however, did not affect or lessen her alertness. Her mind was sharp as always, her eyes were clear, her ears functioned without the aid of hearing devices, and her voice was soft and sweet. This was perhaps because she had guarded these senses all her life with special attention. They were well preserved because they had served only for virtuous purposes. Otherwise she felt extremely weak. Indeed the body would have succumbed long before were it not for her soul's clinging fast to it, unwilling to depart.

A Day Made to Order

During those difficult weeks it was Rochel, Rav Nissim's youngest daughter, who kept watch over her grandmother. Her older sisters had already taken their turn. Tzipora, the eldest, had spent several years with Rebbetzin Batya. Soon after she married, the next in line took charge; and so it went until Rochel became eligible for the coveted responsibility. Reb Nissim's daughters valued greatly the opportunity to serve Rebbetzin Batya. Every minute with their grandmother was a special *zechus* and a cherished lesson for life.

On Sunday, the 24th day of Sivan, 1984, Rebbetzin Batya woke

162 / SILENCE IS THY PRAISE

with unusual energy. Rochel, as well as later visitors who chanced upon the scene, marveled at her sudden rejuvenation. The thrill of being able to translate into activity, albeit on a limited scale, signals to her muscles was a refreshing experience, so much so, that Rebbetzin Batya inadvertently donned her Shabbos dress that morning. It must have been the first time in her life that she had worn her Shabbos dress on a weekday. Nobody drew her attention to the mistake. Perhaps it was a mistake that was meant to be. Certainly the day was special.

At noon, Rebbetzin Leah arrived to serve her mother-in-law a light lunch and then returned to her apartment. While she was eating, Rav Nissim entered. His practice was to visit his mother daily and pay his respects. This was a self-imposed obligation he would not forego, regardless of how full his schedule happened to be. On this occasion he was relieved to find his mother a bit stronger. As always, he exchanged kind words with her. She in turn thrilled with the nearness of her son's Torah wealth.

While Rebbetzin Batya finished her meal, Rav Nissim under-took to rest a bit in the apartment. He often found there a welcome refuge and brief respite from the many people who constantly followed him about from early morning to the late hours of the night in quest of advice, taxing his time mercilessly. Sure enough, it was not long before a man, looking desperate, entered the apartment and asked nervously:

"Is Reb Nissim here? I need his advice urgently."

"Rav Nissim is here," she answered sympathetically. "He is resting at the moment."

The man went on to explain the gravity of the situation. The rebbetzin offered to peek in to see if possibly Rav Nissim was still awake. To help this man was more important to her than her son's badly needed rest. In her concern, she completely forgot that she had been unable for some time to move about unaided, and she made it to the bedroom and back on her own. When it was over, the experience was to her as marvelous as that of a child taking its first steps.

Soon after Rav Nissim left, Rochel returned from Rav Wolf's

Rav Nissim Karelitz followed by people in need of advice

Bais Yaakov Seminary to tend to her grandmother the rest of the day.

At about four in the afternoon, a young newlywed couple arrived unexpectedly. Josepha, Rav Chaim Swiatycki's daughter from Monsey, New York, came to introduce her husband, Avraham Mordechai Schwartz, to her great-aunt, Tante Bashl. The couple hoped also to have their newly established union blessed.

Rebbetzin Batya was elated by the company. The granddaughter of her late sister, Enya Chaya, and her husband were indeed important guests. They were very dear to her. As she exchanged words with them in Yiddish, her inner excitement was visible. As always, however, there was an all-important question in her mind.

"Where does the young man learn?" she wanted to know. Then, turning to Josepha, she added pensively, "If only you knew your grandparents! If only you knew your grandfather, Rav Abba Swiatycki! Oh, he was a great man — truly great. He lived only for Torah. His whole life was spent learning Torah."

Speaking with the young newlyweds aroused in Rebbetzin Batya a longing for Kossova and old times. But true to character, she did not dwell long on the past. Instead her thoughts reverted quickly to the here and now and the foreseeable future. Dreamingly she said, "*Mashiach* is on the way! Don't you see? He is so near." She continued in an air of tender urgency: "We must speed his coming. We must learn Torah. Ask the young Jews in America to learn Torah full time. I am sure my nephew, your father, Reb Chaim, learns Torah day and night. Yes, it can be done in America as well. We must do our utmost in these final moments by learning Torah. We must help *Mashiach* come. Don't you see?" she pleaded with a full heart.

When the visitors were about to depart, Rebbetzin Batya accompanied them to the small porch at the entrance to the apartment. As was her custom, she lingered there until the couple was out of view, showering them with blessings as they left.

The visit of the newlyweds brought to Rebbetzin Batya's mind a replay of her entire past. Among other things, she recalled her own grandmother, Yuspa, the beautiful woman who desired only to follow her mother's ways. It was after Bobbe Yuspa that Josepha was named. Suddenly, however, the glimpse into her past made way for a glorious vision of the future, as again she contemplated the imminent coming of *Mashiach*. Rochel sat near her grandmother, spellbound, absorbing thoughts shared by the two of them.

The past and future were always part of Rebbetzin Batya's present. She was gifted with a special ability to blend them all into perfect harmony. On the 24th day of Sivan the review of her entire life's past coupled with the dream of a magnificent future. Both the review and the dream accompanied her to eternity. It was her last day on earth.

❀ ❀ ❀

AFTER THE *SHLOSHIM*, RAV NISSIM'S FAMILY moved from their old, two-room, two-kitchen apartment on Rav Blau Street to the

A Flask of Pure Olive Oil

Ramat Aharon section of Bnei Brak. His congregants insisted that he live in their midst. It was they who, several years earlier, had arranged for the acquisition of a more spacious and modern apartment on Rebbe Meir Street to house Rav Nissim's family.

Rebbetzin Leah, however, had never been too keen on leaving her old quarters. She had lived in the same tiny apartment since the day of her marriage and was sentimentally attached to the home where her children were born and raised. Very much like her mother-in-law, she was content with little and did not look for modern improvements. Furthermore, their residence on Rav Blau Street had been of great benefit to Rebbetzin Batya, whose apartment was only a flight below. She thus had the advantage of the privacy of her own home while at the same time enjoying the constant care and attention of her distinguished son and his family. Ultimately, however, the family yielded to the wishes of the congregants, and the move was planned.

Most of the furnishings in the old apartment were worthless. Surely the new quarters on Rebbe Meir Street called for a lighter and fresher decor. There was, however, one old piece of furniture the family would not think of leaving behind. This was a unique closet. What could be so special about a shabby, homemade, wooden closet?

Rav Yaakov Yisroel Kanievsky, the Steipler Gaon, had many years earlier learned of the need for a closet in the family. His daughter Ahuva was then about to be married to Rav Shlomo Berman. Due to the lack of funds, it looked as if the newlyweds would have to do without a clothes closet. Rebbetzin Miriam Kanievsky was considerably distressed by this fact. Her husband, the rav, sensed her anguish and wished to lighten her concern. Without ado the Steipler purchased a few boards and the necessary hardware and in no time at all assembled a portable closet with his own hands. Meanwhile a generous relative presented the newlyweds with a brand new closet. Shortly thereafter Rebbetzin Miriam happened to pay a visit to her nephew, Rav Nissim, and his young wife Leah. She noticed that linen, clothing and other household items were kept in an assortment of cartons, apparently for lack of a better storage facility. She immediately offered the young couple the Steipler's homemade closet. Rebbetzin Batya deeply appreciated her sister's generous gift to her children, not only because of its practical use but even more so for the inherent *kedushah* she attributed to it. It was obvious to her that every effort in its construction, every nail hammered into it had been accompanied by profound thoughts of Torah. In this, Rav Nissim's family concurred. This closet is a cherished heirloom in the Ramat Aharon apartment.

🦋   🦋   🦋

The first joyous occasion in the family after Rebbetzin Batya's passing, was the birth of a baby boy to Sara and Oren Austern four months later. The *bris milah* took place in the new apartment on Rebbe Meir Street.

Among the many relatives and friends who assembled for the *simchah* was Rebbetzin Chaya Kopfshitz, the great-grandmother of the baby. She had special cause to rejoice. The child was named after her late husband, Rav Zvi Kopfshitz. Rebbetzin Chaya was gladdened by the tribute her family paid her late husband, not realizing how much her pride in his memory contributed to that end as well. The men gathered in Rav Nissim's dining room for the *seudas mitzvah*. The women were served in the living room of an adjacent apartment. As they were not within earshot of the *divrei Torah*, they turned to Rebbetzin Chaya, requesting that she say a few words. It was well known to everyone present that

Rebbetzin Chaya possessed a repertoire of fascinating stories waiting to be told. She readily agreed.

"Once there was a great king," she began. No elaboration was necessary. Everybody was familiar with the king. "This great king had an extremely loyal and devoted servant." Everyone knew the servant as well.

"Although the king was quite fond of this servant, he nevertheless wished to test the degree of his devotion. He called for the servant and presented him with a small flask of pure olive oil, and said, 'I want you to circle the earth with this flask of oil. I order you to guard it with your life. The road will not be easy. Robbers may attack you in the dread of night, and beasts may threaten your well-being. Yet you must guard this flask of oil at all costs. Moreover, do not dare dilute it or attempt to improve upon it. It is to be kept in the same state of purity as on the day you received it. Your reward will of course be commensurate with your efforts.'

"The servant swore allegiance to his king and left the palace with the flask in hand eager to fulfil his mission. But the undertaking was far from simple. Time and again he encountered hardships on his way. He was attacked by marauders and pursued by wild beasts. The elements were harsh as well. Although his very life was often at risk, he nonetheless guarded the flask with every ounce of wit and strength his being could muster. He resisted a variety of temptations and enticements, especially in the big cities through which he passed. He aimed only to fulfill his sacred mission and to comply with his king's wishes.

"At the end of long years of wandering and after suffering many trials and tribulations, the servant returned to the palace of his master, the king. The oil in the flask had remained intact. It was as pure as on the day it had been presented to him."

All present understood well the parable. Olive oil is a well-known symbol of Torah. The loyal servant had guarded and protected Hashem's Torah with superhuman devotion as he journeyed through life and all its vicissitudes.

The seemingly simple parable had a profound and moving

effect. The wound which the family had suffered four months earlier was still fresh. Rebbetzin Batya's presence was sorely missed. Of all the stories in Rebbetzin Chaya's repertoire, none reflected more on Rebbetzin Batya's life. None was a more fitting tribute to her memory as a faithful servant of the king.

❀ ❀ ❀

"The world stands on three pillars: Torah, service of Hashem and the practice of kindness" (*Pirkei Avos* 1:2).

The Legacy IN THE PROMOTION AND PERFORMANCE of these ideals, the Karelitz family were prominent and peerless builders. The city of Bnei Brak uniquely reflects their spirit and stands in our own time as living and dramatic testimony of their far-reaching impact and influence. Even the physical appearance of the city bears traces of the Karelitz modesty, simplicity and *kedushah*.

There are few commonplace distractions to be found in Bnei Brak. There is little that may attract the eye or lure the senses. It is a city barren of natural beauty. It contains no structures of architectural note. There are no broad avenues, spacious wooded parks or tree-lined boulevards. The city of 120,000 souls is in a physical sense poor, very much like the Karelitz family was. But in a spiritual sense, Bnei Brak is a city of wealth and opulence. There is probably not a single street or alley in Bnei Brak without a house of prayer or a house of Torah study. It abounds in *shuls*, *shtiebels*, *yeshivos*, *kollelim*, *ch'darim*, Bais Yaakov schools and seminaries for girls.

Nowhere in the world is there so much concentrated Torah learning per square foot. Nowhere in the world is there a city that houses so many gifted and saintly Torah scholars. The spirit of Torah visibly dominates its entire populace. People waiting for buses stand on line with *sefarim* in their hands, absorbed in learning. Time is too precious to waste idly. Doctors and dentists have religious books available for their waiting patients in lieu of popular magazines. The demand for religious books is so great that

Yeshivas Ponevez

Yeshivas Slobodka

Yeshiva Beis Shmaya

Yeshivas Tiferes Moshe

A sampling of the many yeshivos and girls schools in Bnei Brak —
Litvishe, Chassidishe, and Sephardic

Yeshivas Chasidei Belz

Kollel Chazon Ish

Yeshivas Birchas Ephraim

Rav Wolf's Seminary for Girls

Yeshivas Vizhnitz

sefarim stores are to be found everywhere. If the Children of Israel are the "People of the Book," Bnei Brak is surely the "City of the Book."

The Chazon Ish and his brother-in-law, the Steipler Gaon, were known to have been in the habit of learning the night through. Bnei Brak teems with institutions whose lights burn through the night for those students who wish to emulate the *gedolim*. Torah learning continues in Bnei Brak around the clock. It never stops. In Ponevez, for example, Rav Dovid Povarsky, the aged *gaon* and *rosh yeshivah*, habitually enters the *beis medrash* at two o'clock every morning. His learning schedule begins at that hour. Invariably, he finds there young men who have not yet retired from the previous day.

Nearly everyone in Bnei Brak lives in cramped and over-crowded apartments. The uniformly built three and four story buildings are virtually on top of each other. Conditions are such that it is common for a housewife to sneeze in her kitchen and hear her next-door neighbor respond with *"Gesundheit."* Notwithstanding the density, there are few within Bnei Brak who wish to live elsewhere. Real estate values are among the highest in the land. The desire of Orthodox Jews to move to Bnei Brak continues unabated. In great measure this is due to the legacy of the Chazon Ish. Three of his nephews, Rav Nissim Karelitz, Rav Chaim Kanievsky, and Rav Chaim Greineman, continue faithfully the tradition of their forebears. All regularly keep open house into the late hours of night advising the public in matters of *Halachah* and Torah-true living. The stream of people from all walks of life coming and going is endless. Rav Chaim Kanievsky is also approached by many who seek his blessings. Rav Chaim Greineman counsels those in need of medical advice. The selfless services of these and other *gedolim* are provided without remuneration. People near and far avail themselves of their wisdom and expertise.

❧ ❧ ❧

All of Israel looks forward to the coming of Shabbos. Every Friday afternoon, Kol Yisrael's English-language service beams its program called "Thank Goodness It's Friday!" Indeed all of Israel is thrilled with the coming of Shabbos. At 1 p.m. trade and business cease, and the clatter of factory machines is silenced. The entire populace looks forward to the blessings of Shabbos. But there is a world of difference between the manner in which a Torah-true Jew and a freethinker celebrate their day of rest. The irreligious look to fill their Shabbos day with as much physical pleasure as they can cram into it. Their acts of desecration are of no concern to them. They simply do not believe in Shabbos.

The Jews of Bnei Brak observe Shabbos in a vastly different manner. By giving of themselves to Shabbos, they rise spiritually. In such giving they find *brachah* and joy. Thus, late Friday afternoon when the sirens sound to announce the approach of Shabbos, 20,000 women in the same instant light their Shabbos candles. By that time Bnei Brak's gates are closed to the outside world. All traffic ceases. Slowly the streets fill with men and children dressed in their finest. A sea of people walk in all directions to a thousand different houses of prayer. Every street becomes a promenade. Shabbos is ushered in with songs of praise, gratitude and thanksgiving. Shabbos in Bnei Brak from beginning to end is an elevating and beautiful experience that has no comparison anywhere in the world.

Yom Tov too is enriching in the unique message it carries. It is observed in Bnei Brak with spirit and enthusiasm. On Shavuos night the *shuls* and *yeshivos* are packed with men learning Torah until daybreak. It is said:

"Half of Bnei Brak is awake on Shavuos night."

"Oh no! That can't be! Only half?"

"Yes, only half. ALL the men, that is."

Bnei Brak probably contains more bank investors than any city in the world. Thousands pool their resources and savings with family and friends and go into the lending business. Money is lent interest-free on a revolving basis to those in need. These banks, known as *gemachim*,* are to be found in Bnei Brak in impressive

---

* An acronym of the words *gemilus chasadim* — meaning acts of kindness.

numbers. The practice of *chesed* is so contagious that *gemachim* compete with each other for borrowers. This aggressiveness is rooted in the Torah's commandment to lend money. The *Midrash* comments:

> "Every man within Israel who lends money to his friend interest-free, Scripture rewards him as if he kept all the commandments."*

The banking business in Bnei Brak is not confined to loans of money. There are *gemachim* that lend just about everything a poor family may need. There is in Bnei Brak a 48-page booklet cataloguing the numerous and varied materials and services available — all absolutely free of charge. Thus a poor person blessed with a *simchah* may borrow all the tables, chairs, dishes, tablecloths, glasses and silverware he needs to make a party. A mother may avail herself of all kinds of items needed for a baby or child. There is even a bank which provides mother's milk for mothers who for some reason are temporarily short of milk and do not wish to wean their babies. There is one lady who specializes in ready-cooked *arbis* (chickpeas) for a *shalom zachar* in the event a baby boy is born late Friday afternoon. The needy may borrow patterns, wedding gowns, books, cassettes, blankets, tools, drills, ladders, old furniture, wheel chairs, crutches, thermometers, vaporizers, even pacifiers. The list is long and growing. In Bnei Brak one need not be a millionaire to be a banker.

> "These are the things of which man enjoys the fruits in this life, and the stock remains for him in the life to come; namely, honoring one's father and mother, the practice of charity, early attendance at the house of study . . . hospitality, visiting the sick, dowering a bride, accompanying the dead to the gravesite, devotion to prayer, and making peace between man and his fellow. *But the study of Torah equals them all*" (Pe'ah 1:1).

---

* *Midrash Rabbah* 31, from *"Lekach Tov"* on *Parshas Mishpatim.*

Other cities are famous for the production of a particular product. Bnei Brak is known for its production of *bnei Torah*. These are its unsung heroes, the men imbued with the spirit of the Chazon Ish and his successors. These *bnei Torah* are in the main gifted and dedicated young scholars who forsake a life of comfort and leisure in order to serve Hashem full time. Sacrifice and struggle have their rewards. The *zechus* of being blessed with devoted helpmates is one such reward.

The wives of *bnei Torah*, very much like Rebbetzin Batya, are exemplary in their virtue and modesty. Most prefer the pale, natural look to artificial make-up and coloring. Their dresses too are unpretentious; they do not go out of fashion. Most important, however, is their selfless devotion to Torah, family and home. In spite of dire poverty and wild inflation, they manage to raise large families on limited budgets. Indeed, they are totally dedicated to the care of husbands and children. Because mutual respect characterizes their lives, the home is a place where the family lives together in harmony. It is truly *a za shaineh shtub*. Each child is a precious jewel, a blessing from Above. Regardless of the size of the family, these wives find time for *hachnasas orchim* and generally do *chesed* whenever and wherever possible. They teach, shop, cook, bake and sew, knit, mend and patch. Evenings, when the work load is done, many muster the strength to attend *shiurim*. Here they learn how further to enrich, refine and beautify a sublime way of life. Here they learn that "she that dwells within the home apportions the spoils" (*Tehillim* 68:13).

This was the legacy Rebbetzin Batya received from her mother, which she apportioned to her children and grandchildren for the lasting benefit of *Klal Yisrael*. By so drawing on her heritage and faithfully transmitting it to posterity, Rebbetzin Batya fulfilled her calling.

❧ Glossary

Glossary

aleph-beis: the Hebrew alphabet

Am Yisrael: the nation of Israel

apikorsim: heretics

avreichim: acronym for *"av b'chachmah rach b'shanim"* ("great in wisdom though young in years"); refers to *kollel* students

baal chesed: a habitual doer of charitable acts

baal tzedakah: a habitual giver of charity

bachurim: young men (usually refers to unmarried *yeshivah* students)

Baruch Hashem: Thank G-d

bas bayis: a guest who so frequents the home that she is like a member of the family

beis din *(batei din,* pl.): religious court

Beis Hamikdash: the Holy Temple in Jerusalem

beis medrash: the study hall of a *yeshivah* or *kollel*

besoros tovos: good tidings

b'ezras Hashem: with G-d's help

Bircas Hamazon: Grace After Meals

bishleimus: perfectly

bissel: (Yiddish) a little

bnei Torah: Torah students

brachah: a blessing

bris milah: a circumcision

challah: braided loaf of bread, used for the Sabbath and festivals

chalutzim: pioneers

chareidi *(chareidim,* pl.): Torah observant, G-d-fearing Jew

chasan: bridegroom

chassidim: followers of a chassidic Rebbe

chavrusa: study partner

Chazal: acronym for *"Chachameinu zichronom livrachah,"* our Sages of blessed memory

cheder *(ch'darim,* pl.): elementary school equivalent, where religious studies are the basic curriculum and little secular education is given

chesed: kind deeds

chevrah: club, league

chiddushei Torah: original comments on the Torah and Talmud

chilonim: secular Jews; Jews who unfortunately did not merit to receive a Torah education

chinuch: education

chofesh hagadol: long vacation

chupah: canopy under which a Jewish marriage ceremony takes place

churban: destruction of the holy Temple in Jerusalem

chutzpah: audacity

daven: pray

derech: way (*baderech*: on the way)

derech eretz: good manners; proper behavior

dvar Torah (*divrei Torah*, pl.): a comment on an area of Torah study, delivered orally or in writing

Eidah Chareidis: (lit., the G-d-fearing congregation) a community of Torah-observant Jews in Jerusalem

eishes chayil: woman of accomplishment

emes: truth

esrog: a citron, one of the four species taken on the Sukkos holiday

eved Hashem: a loyal servant of the L-rd

ezras nashim: the women's section of a synagogue

frum: Torah observant

gadol (*gedolim*, pl.): Torah giant

gadol hador: the greatest Torah personality of the generation

gashmius: materialism

hachnasas orchim: hospitality to guests

hakaras hatov: gratitude

Haskalah: so-called Enlightenment, a movement that opposed traditional Torah life

hasmadah: diligence

havdalah: prayer recited at the close of Sabbath and festivals

hespeidim: eulogies

hisorerus: (lit., awakening) words which will "awaken" the listener and influence him to repent and come closer to Hashem

kallah: bride

kashrus: Jewish dietary laws

kavod: honor

kavod habriyos: the honor of fellow human beings

kedushah: holiness

kibbutzim: collective settlements

kiddush Hashem: sanctification of G-d's Name

Klal Yisrael: the people of Israel

Kohanim: those of the priestly family; descendants of Aharon Hakohen

kollel (*kollelim*, pl.): institution for higher Torah learning attended by young married scholars

kvatter: at a *bris milah*, one who brings the baby to his father to be circumcised

kvatterin: woman who brings baby boy to his circumcision

lashon hara: derogatory speech

lishmah: for the sake of Heaven

Litvak, Litvishe: of, or pertaining to people or customs of Lithuanian origin

maaser: tithes; a tenth of the profits which Jews are obligated to give to charity

machateneste: (Yiddish) the mother-in-law of one's married offspring

"macher": (Yiddish) "doer," most often used sarcastically or humorously

madregah: spiritual level

maggidim: public speakers who arouse the populace to repentance and good deeds, often traveling from city to city to speak

mashgiach: spiritual director of a yeshivah

Mashiach: the Messiah (may he come speedily in our days!)

Maskilim: devotees of *Haskalah*

masmidim: diligent scholars

mazal: good fortune

meidele: (Yiddish) little girl

meiselach: (Yiddish) stories

melamdim: educators of the young

middah *(middos,* pl.): character traits

misnagdim: those opposed to the chassidic movement

mitzvah *(mitzvos,* pl.): a positive or negative Torah commandment

mizbei'ach: the Temple altar

mussar: the study of ethics and moral teachings

mussar vort: (lit., "a word of *mussar"*) a comment dealing with *mussar* topics

nachas: sense of satisfaction

negel vasser: the ritual washing of the hands upon arising from sleep

niftar: deceased

payos: sidelocks of hair

posek: a Rabbinic scholar who is qualified to rule on questions of *halachah*

p'sak halachah: a halachic decision

rebbi (pl. *rebbai'im,* pl.): instructor

rechilus: telling someone that another person said or did something against him

refuah sheleimah: a complete recovery

Ribbono Shel Olam: Master of the universe

Rosh Chodesh: the first day of the new month

rosh yeshivah: the head of a *yeshivah*

ruchnius: spirituality

sefarim: books (usually refers to holy works)

sefer Torah *(sifrei Torah,* pl.): Torah scroll

segulah: good omen

seudah: meal

seudas mitzvah: a meal celebrating the fulfillment of a *mitzvah*

Shacharis: the morning service

shalom zachar: celebration upon the birth of a newborn boy held on the Friday night following the birth (traditionally, chickpeas are served)

shalosh seudos or **seudah shlishis:** the third meal partaken of on Shabbos

she'eilah: question pertaining to *halachah*

sheitel: wig

Shemoneh Esrei: the silent prayer recited three times daily

sheva brachos: (lit., seven blessings) the festive meals to which the bride, groom, and guests are invited during the entire week following the wedding

shidduch: an engagement to marry; a proposed match

shiurim: Torah discourses

shivah: the seven-day mourning period

shlichus: a mission assigned by G-d

shlita: acronym for *sheyichyeh l'yomim tovim aruchim,* may he live a good and long life

shloshim: the thirty-day mourning period

Sh'ma: the Torah selections accepting G-d's kingship and commandments, recited during the morning and evening services, upon retiring at night and before death

shmiras Shabbos: Sabbath observance

shochet: slaughterer of cattle and fowl for meat (according to halachic specifications)

shomrei mitzvos: *mitzvah* observers

shtetl: (Yiddish) town

shtiebel: (Yiddish) chassidic place of worship

shul: a synagogue

siddur: a prayerbook

simchah *(simchos,* pl.): a joyous occasion

talmid chacham *(talmidei chachamim,* pl.): Torah scholar

talmidim: students

tefillin: phylacteries; small leather boxes, containing verses of the Torah, worn by Jewish men during the *Shacharis* service on weekdays

Tehillim: the Book of *Psalms*

tena'im: celebration of an engagement to marry

tinokos shel bais rabban: (lit., children studying at their teacher's home) *cheder* students

treifah: non-kosher

tzaddik *(tzaddikim,* pl.): a righteous person

tzedakah: charity

tzidkus: righteousness

tznius: modesty (in dress and general behavior)

vasser: (Yiddish) water

yahrzeit: Hebrew date of death, commemorated yearly by the family of the deceased

Yamim Noraim: the High Holidays

yarmulke: skullcap

yeshivos ketanos: preparatory divisions of the *yeshivos,* usually attended by students aged 13-17

yesomah: orphan girl

yichus: lineage

Yiddishe mamme: Jewish mother

Yiddishe simchah: Jewish celebration

Yiddishkeit: Judaism

yiras shamayim: fear of Hashem; piety

yishuv: settlement in *Eretz Yisrael*

Yom Tov *(Yamim Tovim,* pl.): Festival

zechus: merit